Real Wealth

BY JONATHAN ROBINSON

BOOKS

The Experience of God
How 40 Well-Known Seekers Encounter the Sacred
(formerly titled *Bridges to Heaven*)

The Little Book of Big Questions
200 Ways to Explore Your Spiritual Nature

Instant Insight
200 Ways to Create the Life You Really Want

Communication Miracles for Couples
Easy Ways to Create More Love and Less Conflict

Real Wealth
A Spiritual Approach to Money and Work

VIDEOS

Intimacy and Sexual Ecstasy
60 Minutes to a Smoke-Free Life

AUDIOS

Real Wealth One-Day Seminar (4 tapes)
The Ten-Minute Pure Love Meditation
Seven Secrets to Greater Happiness
Playful and Passionate Relationships

Please visit the Hay House Website at: **www.hayhouse.com**

Real Wealth

A SPIRITUAL APPROACH TO MONEY AND WORK

JONATHAN ROBINSON

Hay House, Inc.
Carlsbad, CA

Copyright © 1998 by Jonathan Robinson

Published and distributed in the United States by:
Hay House, Inc., P.O. Box 5100, Carlsbad, CA 92018-5100
(800) 654-5126 • (800) 650-5115 (fax)

Edited by: Jill Kramer   *Designed by:* Jenny Richards

Library of Congress Cataloging-in-Publication Data

Robinson, Jonathan, 1959–
    Real wealth :   a spiritual approach to money and work   /   Jonathan Robinson.
        p.   cm.
    Includes bibliographical references.
    ISBN 1-56170-455-5   (trade paper)
    1. Wealth—Religious aspects.   2.   Spirituality.   3.   Quality of life—Religious aspects.   4.   Finance, Personal—Religious aspects.
5. Work—Religious aspects.   I.   Title.
BL65.W42R63   1998
241'.68—dc21   97-33512
                                                                    CIP

ISBN: 1-56170-455-5

01 00 99 98   4 3 2 1
First Printing, March 1998

Printed in the United States of America

CONTENTS

ACKNOWLEDGMENTS

I wish to thank Spirit for teaching me the lessons that led to this book. Of course, sometimes God needs people who are willing and able to transmit His/Her lessons and principles. There are several people who have helped me along these lines:

To Justin Gold for showing me it's possible to have a whole new way of relating to money.

To Joyce Walton and Greg Caruso for being a model of doing whatever it takes to follow God's call.

To my four parents for letting me experiment with "alternate lifestyles" without freaking out.

To my partner, Helena, for never forgetting that God and love are more important than money.

To Yvonne Curtis for her title suggestions, and Paul Ehrlich for his great feedback.

To my agent, Joe Durepos, for his friendship and support.

To my brother, Gary, for helping me through the legal stuff, and

To Jill Kramer at Hay House for wonderful editorial assistance.

INTRODUCTION

This is not just another book about "prosperity conscious-ness." Most books that talk about spirituality and finances primarily discuss how to make more money by changing your beliefs about it. While this book also includes such ideas, it is essentially a book about how to use money and work to be clos-er to Spirit (or God—whatever term you prefer). I believe that by integrating money and work with our spiritual paths, we can become more loving, creative, and fulfilled in our day-to-day lives. We can experience "real wealth."

My journey of learning a spiritual approach to money and work began by spending almost ten years in spiritual communes. Toward the end of this phase of my life, I wound up living in a 1967 Dodge van, often meditating ten hours a day. When I wasn't meditating, I would work odd jobs to have enough money to pay for food. My efforts to dive deeply into my soul eventual-ly led to a wonderful connection with God. Then one day while I was meditating, the "still, small voice within" gave me a message that changed everything. To my surprise, it "suggested" that I do a video about having a successful intimate relationship. Unfortunately, at the time I knew nothing about video produc-tion, marketing, or starting or running a business. To add insult to injury, my girlfriend chimed in that I also knew nothing about having an intimate relationship! But the inner calling to make the video was persistent.

After a little research, I soon discovered that it was going to cost $45,000 to make the video I had in mind. Up to this point in my life, I'd never had more than $2,000 to my name, so I figured that raising such a large amount of money was going to be diffi-cult. To meet the challenge, I knew I would need to drastically change my beliefs and relationship with money. After all, I had previously associated money with being greedy and selfish, and I could see that this perception was going to interfere with my new "mission" to get the video made.

By reading various books, attending financial seminars, and practicing self-hypnosis, I began to change my attitude and beliefs about money. With specific tools that I will reveal in this book, I soon became passionate about entering the material world as a spiritual being. In six weeks I raised the entire $45,000 to make the video, despite the fact I had started with no money or collateral. (In chapter 7, I will go into more detail about how I manifested this sum of money.) The video eventually became the best-selling educational video in America in 1991. Even *Newsweek* did an article about it. My career was launched. I now had the experience of how Spirit can be a wonderful business partner.

Since my experience with the video, I've gone on to several other successful ventures in the material world. While it may look on the outside as if I'm just another businessman, on the inside I have tried to make Spirit my partner in each of the projects I've worked on. Gradually, I've learned that what one does for work can be a path to deepen one's connection to the heaven within.

I should point out that the road has not always been easy for me. I have managed to fall into many of the same money and work traps that other people get caught up in. Yet, I have also been fortunate enough to climb out of these traps and get back on track. My hope is that the ideas and techniques outlined in this book will help you in merging the worlds of money, work, and spirit. When what we do for our livelihood is meaningful and in alignment with our spiritual nature, it feels wonderful. In addition, it gives us many more opportunities for spiritual growth. After all, the typical American works almost 50 hours a week. When our work becomes *part* of our spiritual path—rather than separate from it—our lives start to feel more whole, peaceful, and purposeful.

In essence, a spiritual approach to money and work means that you learn how to make and use money in a way that deepens your experience of Spirit. (Throughout this book, the words *Spirit, God,* and *soul* will be used interchangeably.) It also means that you can learn how to live peacefully and lovingly in the material world—whether you have a large bank balance or not.

In this book, the best of what I've learned from my own experience and from others' wisdom will be covered. I offer quite a few ideas, points of view, and specific methods. You may find that you agree with some and not others. That's fine. I recognize that each person needs different ideas and tools to help him or her take the next step in their personal journey. As you read, your job will be to *act* on the ideas that you feel apply to you at this time in your life, and overlook those that don't apply to your current situation. If you do that, I know that you'll find great value in the principles discussed here.

Making a living need not be a worry or a burden. It need not be something you do separate from becoming a more loving, spiritual person. It can be a fun, challenging, and even *sacred* adventure. I wish you the best on your journey.

— **Jonathan Robinson**

PART ONE

Clearing the Path

CHAPTER ONE

MAKING MONEY TO FEED YOUR SOUL

> *"Prosperity is only an instrument to be used,*
> *not a deity to be worshiped."*
> — Calvin Coolidge

Most of us have heard the adages: "Money can't buy you happiness," "Money can't buy you love," and even "Money is the root of all evil."

Actually, these sayings only apply to those who don't know how to shop properly. Money *can* buy you happiness. Money *can* buy you love. Money can even be the root of all the good you do. It all depends on how you *use* money and what your relationship to it is. If you want, you can use money to buy an ounce of cocaine and fry your brain. On the other hand, you can use money to take spiritual-growth workshops and contribute to people in great need. Money is simply a magnifier of you and what you find truly meaningful. If you value the pursuit of enlightenment or a deeper connection with Spirit, money can be a wonderful tool to accelerate your journey—*if* you use it properly.

Whether we like it or not, the pursuit of money and the importance of it in our lives seems to be here to stay. We can complain about how significant it has become, or we can even try to deny its importance. Yet, the truth is that money affects almost every area of our lives, including our relationship with Spirit. In order to align our pursuit of money with our spiritual aspirations, several things must be learned and understood. First and foremost, we need to know *why* we want more money in our lives. Is it to buy meaningless material objects that distract us from our true purpose? Hopefully not. Do we desire money to becomea better, more "spiritual" person? Hopefully yes. But if we are to use money to become "more spiritual," then we need to define exactly what being spiritual means to us.

I think there are some helpful clues that can point us in the right direction. One such clue can be found by listening to what people who have had near-death experiences (NDEs) say about the ultimate purpose of human life. Many years ago, I had my own close encounter with death after an auto accident. During my NDE, I was surprised to find that I was "asked" to evaluate my life based on two questions. After this experience, I talked to dozens of people who also had an NDE—and found that most of them were asked to evaluate their life based on the *same* two questions. The first question is "What did you learn about love?" The second question is "How well did you use your gifts to contribute to other people and the world?"

I think it's more than just coincidence that the themes of love and contribution come up so frequently for people close to death. These concepts are also echoed in almost every spiritual tradition the world has ever known. If these two ideas really *do* point to our purpose as human beings, how can money help us achieve these goals more quickly and effectively? I believe that the first step is to formulate a plan detailing exactly *how* we could use additional money to be more loving, giving individuals, and how money might help us form a deeper connection with Spirit.

Before discussing how money might be used in altruistic ways, first consider what you currently associate with the idea of money. Here's a test for you: Think about what it would be like to manifest and possess a tremendous amount of money. Before reading ahead, take a moment to imagine such a fate and how it would change your life.

When you envision making and having a lot of money, what do you see? For some people, wealth represents freedom, generosity, and peace of mind. For others, it means buying a lot of possessions, long hours at work, greed, and paying higher taxes. Because we all grow up in different environments, each person has a different idea about what having a lot of money would be like. Since my childhood experiences with respect to money were mostly negative, I had emotional blocks to making a lot of it. My bank account simply reflected my subconscious mind.

Most people have both positive and negative associations to money. While we may *believe* that we only have positive thoughts about it, our subconscious mind may have picked up some highly negative beliefs. We may have heard our parents being judgmental about "rich folks," or subconsciously noticed that having more money never really changed things in our family. Like two hands pushing against each other, these conflicting feelings about money may have resulted in a lot of effort, without much net effect. After all, the subconscious mind is always trying to steer us clear of emotional pain and difficulty. If there are any hidden negative judgments you associate with being wealthy, you'll subconsciously avoid financial abundance.

While living in my 1967 Dodge van, making $300 a month, I reviewed all the negative thoughts I had about having a lot of money. To me, being financially abundant was "unspiritual," and spiritual growth was the most important thing in my life. No wonder I wasn't rich. Yet, now that the "still, small voice within" had given me a task involving money (making a video), I took on the chore of clearing out the obstacles in my mind.

To accomplish this aim, I made the following list, stating how money would help me achieve what was truly important to me:

Ten Things That Are Really Important to Me

1. Inner peace and meditation
2. Becoming the best person I can be
3. Being happy
4. Traveling around the world
5. Personal and spiritual growth
6. Making the world a better place
7. Being in a great relationship
8. Spending quality time with friends
9. Having fun
10. Having a nice place to live

I suggest that you make up a similar list of five to ten things that are really important to you. After making my list, I simply wrote down how an abundance of money could help me "move forward" with each item. Part of what I wrote was the following:

With an abundance of money, I could take various workshops that could further my professional and spiritual development. I could spend time with various spiritual teachers and find out their best ideas and methods for experiencing Spirit. I could travel to exotic lands and learn things that might really make a difference in my own life—and perhaps in the lives of others.

It would be great to visit places such as India, Europe, Israel, and New Zealand. I've always wanted to see the Taj Mahal by the light of the full moon. India has various spiritual teachers I'd like to visit. It would be fantastic to climb a glacier in New Zealand.

Having an abundance of money would allow me to take great care of my body. I could eat more nutritionally and take more time for needed rest, relaxation, and meditation. By taking really great care of my physical health, I'd be better equipped to meet the personal challenges and opportunities that come my way. In addition, I'd be more able to contribute something valuable to other people and the planet.

With more money, I would have time and energy to pursue the projects and causes I feel most strongly about. I'd be able to complete the two books I've been thinking about, and possibly help inspire more people. I wouldn't have to worry about money so much, which would free up my life so I could spend more quality time with Helena [my partner], other people I love, and with Spirit in moments of prayer and meditation.

If I were richer, I'd feel better about myself—not because my worth is to be judged by money, but because having money would mean I've more fully expressed who I am in the world. It would indicate that I've been willing to use the gifts I've been given to contribute to others, learn from my mistakes, and not settle for a life of mediocrity.

This was a shortened form of what I originally wrote to link money to the things I truly value in life. I suggest that you write a similar essay. If you don't know for sure what you'd like to do with more money, then you're putting out the message that you're not quite ready for it yet. I know you don't *want* to sit down and write, but would you write a brief essay for $1,000? If you answer yes, then let me assure you that the financial and spiritual benefits you could reap from writing down these thoughts will be far greater than $1,000. The more graphic and specific you can make your essay, the better. To say you'd like to travel is one thing, but to mention all the wonderful sights you'd like to see is much more compelling.

An alternative to writing something down is to simply tell a friend how having more money could enrich your life. Once again, it's important that you be specific about how ten, fifty, or five hundred thousand extra dollars could improve the quality of your life. By stating these thoughts out loud or by reading your "money essay," you will be more motivated to pursue your monetary (and related) dreams. In addition, by planning in advance exactly how you'd spend your wealth, you'll be conditioned to spend it wisely when the extra dollars start rolling in.

If you are in a huge amount of debt, you might pay off some of it with the extra money you'll soon be making, but make sure you always use some percentage of your money to nourish your soul. As a result, you'll create a sense of alignment within yourself, allowing the spiritual and worldly part of you to work in harmony toward a common goal. When our minds and hearts are working in perfect alignment, miracles, synchronous events, and enjoyable moneymaking opportunities seem to magically appear.

Pass the Buck

In my *Real Wealth* seminars, I play a little game called "Pass the Buck." It's a very interesting game with a powerful point, so I'll explain it to you. The game consists of the following instructions:

1. Take an amount of money out of your wallet that you'd be willing to lose—or win.

2. When I say "go," you will have four minutes to give money to others or receive money from others as often as you would like. You must make at least one pass with the money you have in your hand right now.

3. At the end of four minutes, I'll say "stop," and what you have in your hand will be yours.

The lack of absolute clarity in the instructions is intentional. Just like the "money game" in real life, how to play and how to "win" the "Pass the Buck" game is not completely clear. Since the rules are a bit nebulous, people tend to play this game in the same way they handle money situations in their own lives. I always refuse to answer questions, so the participants are forced to play a game in which they are not confident about the rules. Once I say that I won't answer any questions, the game immediately begins.

As people begin the game, I also join in on the festivities. After giving my dollar away, and usually getting a dollar or five dollars in return, I ask various people if I can have the money in their hands. Normally, they say yes. I then proceed to take their money without giving them any in return. Once in a while, someone will protest and say, "Hey, *I* want something in return!" If they say this, I give them one dollar and move on to the next person, repeating this process. By the end of the four minutes, I usually have about $90, and most people in the seminar have nothing.

I then ask people to notice how much money they have, and if they have less than what they started with, to explain why. There is usually an uproar of people complaining that I played unfairly because I have almost all the money. Since I've played this game many times, I've come to realize that the excuse that people come up with for losing their money is usually the same excuse they have for not making much money in their own lives. As people yell out their excuses ("I didn't understand the rules!" "This game isn't fair!"), I point out that I played by the exact same rules I spelled out. The reason I end up with most of the money is because I play the game to win—not to look good, avoid embarrassment, or be liked. Unfortunately, when faced with a situation in which the rules aren't totally clear, most people allow fear to guide them. They lose touch with what their own goals, principles, and values are, and instead simply try not to make any mistakes.

Of course, judgments of greed and selfishness start flying at me. At this point, I tell the participants what I plan to do with the money: I send *all* of it to feed starving children in India, a long-time favorite charity I support. This usually shuts people up. I go on to explain that because I *knew* each dollar I collected would feed a starving child for three days, I was willing to play aggressively. Even in situations in which I don't feel confident, I play to win because I feel deserving of the money I make. I know it will be used for a good purpose. I have found that the clearer people are about the purpose of money in their lives, the more they tend to make. Their personal mission becomes more important than trying to avoid mistakes or being judged by others.

Do you have a cause that's worth fighting for? If you don't, your dollars will slip through your hands and into the waiting arms of someone who *does* have a cause he or she believes in. That's why writing your money essay or telling a friend your dreams is so useful. In my *Real Wealth* seminars, I've found that most people simply don't feel deserving of the money they receive; therefore, they are blocked from making any more. It is imperative that whatever you decide to spend money on, you absolutely believe it is a legitimate and holy way of spending that money. If it does not feel that way, then perhaps you need to associate money with causes that have more meaning and depth to you. Once you understand this concept in your gut, you'll be amazed by how much more money ends up in your pockets.

Money Mission Statement and Picture

There's an old legend that states that in the days when St. Peter's Cathedral was being built, a scribe from a nearby town went to interview some of the builders of the mighty church. He saw three bricklayers working hard at their job and asked each of them what they were doing. According to the story, the first bricklayer said with annoyance, "Can't you see what I'm doing? I'm placing this clay and mud in these brick molds, carrying it over there, and then placing it on that wall when it's dry."

The scribe asked the second bricklayer what he was up to, and he replied, "I'm laying bricks so I can support and feed my wonderful wife and two lovely daughters." Finally, the scribe asked the third bricklayer what his job was, and he glowingly reported, "I have the deep honor to get paid to help build the mightiest cathedral of all time. With each brick I lay, I am working to create a miraculous building that will help millions of people experience their connection to the Lord of the Universe! With the money I make, I can help spread the love of Spirit to my family, friends, and all those I meet." Which of these three bricklayers do you think enjoyed his job the most? Which do you think did his job best? Being in touch with your mission at work and the purpose of money in your life has definite advantages.

Since we all can lose track of our deeper purpose while engaged in the material world, I think it's helpful to briefly state why our livelihood is important and how money serves our spiritual growth. In the previous story, bricklayer number three was able to state in 67 words why his job was important and why he deserved the money he made. Creating such a "money mission statement" can help point you in the right direction throughout your day. A money mission statement is simply a very brief reminder of what you write in your money essay. By memorizing your money mission statement, you'll have a convenient tool to help you get back on track if you've lost your way. Sometimes, when I'm trying to decide on a purchase, I refer back to my money mission statement and see if it's "in line" with it. Having read my money essay, you can see how my money mission statement brings it all together in one simple sentence:

"I use money to gain access to the best information, the best health care, and the finest spiritual resources available so I might help myself and others be more loving and more effective in making this world a better place."

It might take you a while to get your money mission statement just right—but it's time well spent. It can become a convenient affirmation for your mind—reminding you of why you deserve money and how you can use money to feed your soul. Along with my money mission statement that I have posted where I can see it each day, I've hung up a photo that reminds me, in a very powerful way, of my money purpose. The picture is of one of the hungry kids I help feed. Sometimes I don't feel like making the extra business calls I know I should make, but the image makes me push past my resistance. What picture could *you* use to remind yourself that the pursuit of money is connected to what is truly most important to you? The more you associate money to such a meaningful concept, the easier it will be to manifest lasting wealth—and use that wealth to nourish your soul.

The Road Less Traveled to Riches

The primary reason people desire money is so they can buy things that will make them feel better. In essence, money is simply an indirect way of buying feelings we like. A person buying a Rolls Royce wants to feel respected, secure, and proud. A person going to a James Bond film is "buying" the feelings of excitement and adventure. However, the things that people normally buy with money only lead to ephemeral pleasures. As a culture, we've been hypnotized to believe that buying a luxury car is a more effective way to feel satisfaction than having a deeper experience of Spirit. That's why a major part of a spiritual approach to money is learning to use money to become a more peaceful, loving, and joyful person. Using money in this manner will not result in the "instant high" of buying some new clothes or gadgets, but it will ultimately lead to a deeper experience of what one truly values.

I believe "real wealth" means that people experience very little worry or frustration in their lives, and instead feel a lot of joy, love, peace, and freedom. While money *can* be used to help a person evolve spiritually, it's important to remember that it is not as necessary as we've been led to believe. Most people would agree that Jesus and the Buddha experienced real wealth, yet they lived with almost no money at all. The truly important things in life already exist within the human heart. The more we can *remember* what's really important in life and the more we can tap into the peace and love within, the "wealthier" we become.

As I've previously mentioned, I spent three years living in a van. During this time, I worked a few hours a week and made about $300 a month. Because I had very few expenses, I was actually able to save about $150 a month, and I felt as if I had plenty of money. After all, I was saving over half my income. Instead of spending a lot of money on gadgets and entertainment, I had a lot of fun reading, meditating, and working out at the gym. One day while I was relaxing in the gym spa, a man lamented that he just couldn't make ends meet on $40,000. Since my annual income at the time was under $3,600, I initially found this hard to believe. Yet, he was in obvious pain, so I listened compassionately. He went on to complain about the mortgage on his house, his taxes, and the huge payments he had to make on various possessions he owned. My heart was really feeling for him until he said, "You know, you just can't make ends meet on $40,000 *a month* anymore."

I learned a great lesson that day. I understood that it doesn't matter how much money you make if you don't know how to use it to nourish your soul. I also learned that lessening your desires and indulgences can be a viable road to riches. I currently know of several spiritually evolved people who have managed to retire before the age of 40. They have all used the same "secret" method for achieving their early retirement. First, as I explained earlier in this chapter, they associated making money with what they really valued. Then, while the money was rolling in, they continued to live a simple life. They learned to feel love, joy, and peace without having to buy expensive items or live in an extravagant home. Since they had few needs, they were able to save a lot of money. With their extra money, they made investments and eventually managed to live off the income from those investments.

The ability to be flexible in how we get what we want in life can be of enormous value in our efforts to become wealthy. For example, in order to feel peace of mind, some people need to buy a house in the country, take a long vacation, or have a million dollars in the bank. Yet, a less needy or more spiritually evolved person could simply close his or her eyes and meditate. Although a country house and a day of meditation can both lead to peace, the day of meditation costs significantly less. That's why before making big purchases it's a good idea to ask yourself, "Is there any less expensive way I might experience more of what I ultimately want?" Becoming skilled at finding love, peace, and joy in the little moments of daily life can save you a lot of money.

To become efficient in getting what you really want, it's necessary that you not only master how you spend your money, but also how you spend your time. In recent years, many people have experienced a new form of poverty—the feeling of never having enough time. Like not having enough money, being "time poor" is largely the result of spending time doing activities that are not deeply satisfying. The experience of spending money or time in superficial ways ultimately leaves people feeling unfulfilled.

Previously, I had you make a list of activities that are truly important to you. Although I suggested that you make this list to remind you to spend your money wisely, you can also use this list to see if you're spending your time pursuing what you really value.

We've all heard the adage, "Time is money." You can quickly become wealthier than most millionaires just by being careful about how you use your time. In my opinion, people who have little money but spend their time wisely are richer than those with a lot of money but little quality time to savor life. When where we spend our time is incompatible with what we truly value in life, we become poor in spirit and unhappy in life. Conversely, as we spend our time in alignment with meaningful activities, we become wealthier. In my own life, I've seen that using my time wisely has often led to many unexpected benefits. First, as I use my time to do what I really value, I inevitably spend less money in my life because I feel more satisfied. And second, when I spend time doing what's important to me, I end up being more receptive to ideas that I can later turn into things that make money!

The alternate roads to wealth are especially suited to spiritual seekers. In order to develop a deeper connection to our soul, we need to learn to enjoy simplicity. As we turn to Spirit, nature, and sharing love with one another in order to feel the way we want, we find that we don't *need* as much money as before. When money or work is slow to come in, we can use our time to pursue other important goals, and still feel at peace because we know how to find the joy within. When money *is* flowing easily, we can rest assured that we can use it to nourish our soul. By staying true to our spiritual path and using money in alignment with our heart, real wealth is practically guaranteed.

෨ ෨ ෨

REAL WEALTH REMINDERS

1. If used properly, money can accelerate your spiritual progress and can help you become a more loving and giving person.

2. To feel more deserving and motivated to create wealth, it's beneficial to write down what's most important in your life, along with an explanation of how having additional money could help you achieve or experience each of these things. By writing a "money mission statement," you can quickly recall how money can serve to nourish your spiritual growth.

3. Wealth can most effectively be achieved by using your money and time wisely, while at the same time learning to reduce your needs. If you can tap into the love, peace, and joy within, then even a little money will be more than you need—and you will have found real wealth.

CHAPTER TWO

THE ALCHEMY OF MONEY

"Where your treasure is, there your heart will be also."
— Matthew 6:21

In the Middle Ages, alchemists supposedly tried to turn lead into gold. Actually, alchemy began as the science of transforming one's lower nature and desires into spiritual qualities—such as love, generosity, and inner peace. In the previous chapter, I talked about the importance of associating money with what you really value. In a way, this is an example of alchemy—converting one's "lower" associations to money into a more spiritual vision of how money can be used. As people enter into this alchemical process, they learn to use money to feed their souls.

The next step in the alchemy of money is to look at how the pursuit of riches can potentially *block* your relationship to Spirit. By clearly acknowledging the ways in which money can corrupt your soul, it's possible to sidestep the most common mistakes people make when pursuing riches. Making a "map" of the various ways people get caught in their lower nature when pursuing wealth is crucial for staying on the right path. The map of "money traps" I'll be presenting in this chapter can help you more easily and quickly recognize when you've veered off course.

As I observed people with a lot of money, I soon discovered that there are *five* specific ways in which having riches can interfere with one's spiritual connection. Although I have, at one time or another, fallen into each of these money traps, my awareness of them has helped me climb out very quickly. I have also discovered that, for each money trap, there is a *corresponding* "spiritual" way of living in the material world.

The pursuit of money or success can be like a "purification fire." It *first* tends to bring up our lower nature. Our mission, should we decide to accept it, is to be aware of how wealth can magnify our lower nature, and instead, use it to *magnetize* us to our *higher* nature. Such is the art of money alchemy. It's perfectly all right to get caught in money traps. It's only by experiencing our shadow side that we have a chance to heal or transcend it. Therefore, for each of the five most common money traps I outline, I discuss how to easily get in touch with the antidote so you can transform your lower desires into a spiritual experience. As you focus on these spiritual ways to handle your money, you'll find you will feel freer, more loving, and more connected to Spirit. With the right awareness, monetary success can be a spiritual growth tool—a modern-day form of yoga!

Trap #1: Never Enough

One of the most common ways in which people get lost on the money treadmill is to think that they never have enough. If the money you currently have in your life could magically enter a human body and talk to you, what might it say? If you're like most people, it would probably say something like this: "You never appreciate me. All you ever do is complain about how I'm never enough. You're always worrying about how I might let you down in the future or might totally leave you. I don't feel like you trust me at all. And after all I *do* for you! I'm always getting things for you, protecting you, entertaining you, and making your life easier—but do I ever get a heartfelt thank you? Nooooo!" If we treated our mate the way we "relate" to money, he or she wouldn't want to hang around!

I've created a metaphor that represents why so many people feel like they never have enough—even if they have millions. Imagine trying to fill a gigantic bowl, but no matter how much stuff you put into the bowl, it never fills up. You put a Mercedes in the bowl, a new house, a boat, but it never seems full for more than a few minutes. The reason the bowl never fills up is because it is leaking from the bottom! No matter what you put in, it quickly runs out. You are soon left completely empty.

The bowl represents our desires. In order to get us to keep filling our bowls, television ads and movies tell us *if we only had* (fill in the blank), *then* we'd finally be *full*-filled. But because the bowl has a huge hole in the bottom, we never get to the place where we feel satisfied. When people start acquiring the accouterments of material success, this can sometimes trigger an even *bigger* leak in the bowl of desires. So begins the endless cycle of never feeling like we have enough.

Recently, I experienced this dilemma in a big way, and only my awareness of the problem helped me step off the treadmill. Within a single month, I was featured on *Oprah,* CNN, and the largest radio show in the world for my book *The Little Book of Big Questions.* A week after the *Oprah* show, I called my publisher to see how my book was doing. The man I talked to said it was on the bestseller list and had sold over 90,000 copies in the previous week. Since I made over a dollar per book, I figured I had made about $100,000 and was headed for a lot more money! My mind went wild. I started to think of all the things I could buy and do with this windfall. I'm embarrassed to admit it, but I even began to think thoughts such as, *If I only had $50,000 more, then I could* really *create the lifestyle I've always wanted.* Instead of bringing me more peace, this extra money was leading me to feel an even deeper sense of "not enough."

It turned out that I had been given the wrong information about my book. Instead of 90,000 copies selling after the *Oprah* appearance, it was actually *9,000* copies that sold. In less than a minute, I lost over $80,000! I hung up the phone and absorbed the realization that all the things I had planned to do with this money would not come to be. I laughed at myself for getting so caught up in worrying about what I was going to do with the money, and how it wasn't quite enough to do everything I wanted. Instead, I started feeling grateful for the lesson I was being given. My thoughts turned to how fortunate I was, and I began to feel tremendously wealthy. I laughed at the irony of being told I had $80,000 less than I thought I had, yet feeling richer than I had felt in weeks.

The Antidote: Gratitude

The ability to feel thankful for what we have *right now* can plug up the leak in the bottom of our bowl of endless desires. Through the habit of feeling grateful for the material things in our lives, a whole new energy and experience is created. People often pursue money for years just so they can have a few moments of feeling like they have enough. Yet, the practice of gratitude can make us feel rich faster than any "get rich quick" scheme ever invented. After all, if you feel thankful for what you have, you're immediately rich! But if you have millions and don't appreciate it, then you're *eternally* poor.

Perhaps you're thinking that it would be easy to feel grateful if you only had some more money. If only, if only—the curse of the modern mind. A recent study asked a group of rich, middle-class, and poor folks how much money would be *enough*. Even the rich people surveyed said that they didn't have enough money right now, but if they had just 15 percent more money, THAT would be enough. Of course, when the 15 percent more appears, our needs and desires always seem to rise accordingly. A continual leak in the bowl.

If you own a car, you are automatically in the top 7 percent of wealth of the world. If you don't feel grateful for being in the top 7 percent, being in the top 2 percent won't make much difference. The truth is that you and I live better today than kings lived just 100 years ago! We are blessed with being able to go to the grocery store and choose from 20,000 food items. We are blessed with inexpensive ways to enjoy music, read books, be entertained, talk to people on the phone, and even travel to distant lands. There's a lot we can feel grateful for—if we don't fall into the pothole of "if only" thinking.

I've learned that the discipline of gratitude begins by appreciating whatever you currently have—even if part of you doesn't like it. Feeling grateful, as opposed to feeling like you don't have enough, actually helps to attract money to you. Wouldn't you rather give to someone who appreciated what you gave, rather than someone who always complained that you didn't give enough? If you can tune into feeling wealthy through the practice of gratitude, you'll start to be part of the "grand money flow." In the material world, similar energies attract. When you feel like you don't have enough, you actually push wealth away. Yet, when you feel abundant and grateful, money more easily flows in your direction.

In my own battle with the "not enough" trap, I learned some tools that immediately helped me convert my feelings of scarcity into feelings of abundance and thankfulness. My favorite method is perhaps the simplest: Whenever I notice that I'm thinking that I don't have quite enough, I ask myself the question, "What *could* I feel grateful for?" When I began this practice, I only came up with intellectual answers. Yet over time, I've been able to tune into the actual *feeling* of deep gratitude for the many wonderful things in my life. Gratitude is like a muscle that needs to be exercised. The more I've meditated on this question, the easier it has been to feel truly grateful.

A second approach I've used in order to feel grateful is to compare myself to people less fortunate than I am. When I was in the auto accident that led to my NDE, I remember wondering if I had become paralyzed. As my hands and feet responded to my thoughts, I was overcome with gratitude. Several other people in the van were not so fortunate. Each day I still take time to feel thankful for the use of my limbs.

What blessings have you received that you could feel grateful for? Take a minute now and give your sincere thanks to the Universe or God. With practice, you can tap into the gold mine of gratitude in a moment. . .instant riches, and you don't even have to get off your couch!

A third and final road to gratitude is to simply give verbal thanks for the many blessings in your life. That's what saying grace before a meal does. Yet, it need not apply just to food. We can say a sincere thank you for waking up healthy, ending a safe journey, watching a good TV show—anything. This simple tool can make you feel wealthier than most millionaires. If you practice the discipline of gratitude, you'll avoid the "not enough" treadmill, experience true money alchemy, and enjoy inner riches.

Trap #2: Attachment

A second dynamic of money alchemy is the ability to act without attachment. One of the traditional forms of yoga is called "karma yoga," which is the path of selfless service. In karma yoga, the goal is to act in full alignment with your heart—being of service to others—while at the same time being unattached to the results. When we become too attached to the results we desire, anxiety, fear, and worry are allowed to raise their ugly heads. Our peace of mind is decimated. As we become attached to our money and possessions, each added dollar can feel like a greater burden on our shoulders. In addition, when we become too focused on the results we want to achieve, our ability to listen to Spirit is temporarily lost.

In order to transcend attachment and to experience what I call "letting go," it's important to remember that Spirit cares more about what *kind* of people we are than what we accomplish. As we express our gifts in the world, such as running a company or performing some charitable service, our goal should be to become a more caring, compassionate, and peaceful person. The late Mother Teresa said it best when she stated, "It's not how *much* we give, but how much love we put in the doing." As Westerners, it is extremely difficult to act passionately in the world and yet, at the same time, give the results of those actions over to Spirit.

When I wrote my first book, *Bridges to Heaven*, I got a good lesson in attachment and letting go. I had been working on this book for almost two years and had spent a lot of time, energy, and money interviewing 40 of the foremost spiritual leaders on the planet. After asking people such as Mother Teresa, the Dalai Lama, Ram Dass, Marianne Williamson, Louise Hay, and Wayne Dyer to reveal their personal methods of connecting with God, I went about trying to sell the book to a publisher. To my amazement, I had no luck—and the less luck I had, the more attached to the project I became. Although the book started as a heartfelt way to serve God, I began to burn with the fire of attachment.

Fortunately, my partner, Helena, helped me overcome my self-imposed hurdle. While she and I were camping in the middle of a vast desert, I was obsessing about how all the efforts I had put into MY book were seemingly going to waste. Helena listened to my tale of woe and suggested, "Why don't you just let go and surrender the book for five minutes?" This was a thought that had never occurred to me. It had always seemed like an all-or-nothing proposition. I prayed to let go of my worries and attachment for five minutes and soon felt a wonderful sense of release. Since I felt so good, I decided to "give the book back to God" for an entire month. If the book was still unpublished at that time, I figured I could retake control and continue worrying about it then.

The Antidote: Letting Go

A week after I returned home from the desert, I got a call from a wonderful company interested in publishing the book. I took this as a sign that, by giving the book back to God, I had done what was necessary for the book to become a reality. When we become too attached to a particular result, it seems to block the flow of Grace. Holding on to how we think things should be is tantamount to telling Spirit we know what's best—and don't butt into our lives. Yet, when we let go, it seems to complete a "cosmic circuit" that allows peace to prevail and miracles to happen.

I should point out that letting go does not mean that you should be passive, nor does taking action mean that you are attached. The experience of attachment or letting go is really an internal experience. In Islam they have a saying, "Trust in Allah, but tie your camel." People's external actions may or may not indicate their degree of letting go. Nevertheless, they *feel* completely different. Attachment feels like a contraction of one's being and a fear of the future. It leads to worry and anxiety. On the other hand, letting go leads to feelings of peace, openness, and expansion.

In this culture, we have a lot of courses and books on how to achieve our goals, but we have very little information about *how* to let go and surrender to God's will. Fortunately, there is a science of letting go and giving things back to Spirit. I have found three things to be of particular help in learning the art of surrender. The first thing is knowing the value of it. When we surrender or give things back to God, peace is possible. When we hold on, we are only happy if we get exactly what we want, and what we want is often not the best for others or ourselves in the long term. The simple recognition that holding on leads to suffering is often enough to trigger the thought that it's time to let go. When I find myself pushing for a certain result, I consciously go over in my mind the pain I experience from insisting that things be MY way. I remind myself that, ultimately, I do not know what's best for myself. I remember to trust that there is an intelligence to the Universal plan.

A second thing that helps me let go is prayer. More specifically, I pray to be released from my attachment to a particular result. In a fascinating study by the Spindrift Organization, people were instructed to pray in different ways in order to help plants grow. Some people were instructed to pray that a group of plants would grow big, tall, strong, and healthy. Another group of plants was not prayed for at all. And some people simply prayed "Let thy will be done" to a third group of plants. Guess which group of plants did the best? The plants that were prayed for in the manner of "Let thy will be done" grew faster, taller, and stronger than either of the other groups. This shows that there is power in the art of surrender, in giving things over to God so that Spirit's energy can manifest with the least amount of obstruction from us.

In my prayers of surrender, I simply remind myself of the pain and anxiety I experience from being too attached to a particular result, and ask that I might be released to be a simple servant of God's will. When I finally let go, I often feel a profound level of peace and spiritual energy. It's as if a floodgate has been opened, allowing Spirit to manifest for the highest good of all. I have found the need to surrender and give things back to God to be an ongoing process. It is not something I do once and never have to do again.

The human mind can be sneaky. Even though you may have surrendered a project to God an hour ago, the mind will often try to grab things back and make them go the way you want. To counteract this tendency, I've developed a third method for helping me experience the peace of surrender. I call it the "one-breath technique for letting go." Whenever I realize that I'm starting to get uptight and attached, I take one very deep breath, hold it for about five seconds, and exhale with a loud sigh. In my exhalation, I mentally think, *Let thy will be done.* Sometimes I have to do this simple exercise ten times a day if part of me is persistent in trying to take over how things should be. By practicing these simple tools for letting go, I have found that I am able to experience more peace while acting passionately in the world. In addition, I have found that miraculous results occur more often as I enter into a partnership with the Creator of the Universe.

Trap #3: Selfishness

With an increase in our finances, our selfish nature frequently becomes more apparent. If you only make $15,000 a year, it can be hard to see how you're selfish—since all your money goes toward paying for life's necessities. Yet, when you make $150,000 a year, you get to *see* how you deal with your discretionary income. Does the "extra" money go toward putting a Jacuzzi in your Lear jet? Or does it go toward feeding your soul and being a more generous person? In the alchemy of money, our job is to transform our selfishness and greed into the experience of kindness and generosity.

In order to avoid being trapped in selfishness, I have tried to understand *why* so many people get caught up in it. As I've studied selfish people, I've seen that their behavior is dictated by the fear of not having enough. In an attempt to get enough, they hoard possessions and money. Unfortunately, what they *really* want is more love and respect, but their selfish behavior inevitably leads them to feel even less self-love and self-respect.

As the people they care about withdraw from them, the only thing they know to do is to become even *more* selfish. A vicious cycle of selfishness ensues.

The Antidote: Generosity

To avoid this selfish cycle, I've taken a look at how very generous people live. I've observed that they give frequently, with little or no thought of ever getting anything back. The result is that they become well loved and respected—which results in a greater sense of abundance—which, in turn, leads them to feel free to give even more. Instead of riding a downward cycle of greed and selfishness, generous people float on an upward cycle of love and abundance. So why doesn't everyone attempt to ride the upward cycle? Most people never feel like they have enough love, money, or respect to *begin* this process. They get stuck in the hoarding phase.

To avoid or transcend this major obstacle, several things have helped me. First, writing the "money essay" (from chapter 1) helped me clarify exactly how I could make good use of a higher income. As I read the essay, I began to feel confident that I could really use extra money in a beneficial manner. Next, I decided to start a tithing account in which I gave 10 percent of my money away to worthy causes and people in need. For me, tithing began as a "forced" way to make sure I was generous with my money, but later turned into a very dynamic and sweet way of interacting with Spirit. Since my experiments in tithing had a major effect on me, I have devoted much of an entire chapter to it later in this book.

Giving without attachment to what will come back is a hard thing to do. It's actually a bit scary. It feels like a loss of control, yet that's exactly what generous people learn to do. When I realized this, I decided that as I created more wealth, I would *consciously* start giving as much as possible. That way, I could *use* my increasing wealth to help me consistently experience the grace of being an abundant, generous person. As I've felt better about myself and have had more money, it's become easier. At some point, I reached a "critical mass" of giving in which I saw I was receiving back a lot more than what I gave. From this new feeling of abundance, it has become even easier to give—which has inevitably led to receiving even more. It's a wonderful feeling. Occasionally, when I feel down on myself and I feel a lack of abundance, I still fall victim to the hoarding cycle. Yet, it feels so constricting that I soon do whatever I can to get off that path. Having more money can definitely be invaluable in making the leap from hoarding to helping. The selfish cycle leads to fear, worry, and a type of hell; the experience of being consistently generous leads to love, respect, and overflowing abundance—heaven!

Trap #4: Laziness

Step number four in achieving money alchemy is to be aware of the need to transcend laziness. Many people who make a large amount of money find that they lose their motivation and become lazy. Think about it—if you suddenly won five million dollars in the lottery, how would it change your life? Be honest. You'd probably go on the vacation you've always wanted to take, and then perhaps you'd buy a new car and house. Hopefully you'd use some money to feed your soul or help people in need. But what then? There would still be $4.5 million left. Would you continue to work at your present job? Might you just become a lazy couch potato, sitting at home with nothing to do?

Since Americans generally work a lot of hours, when we think of "making it big," we often think of how we'd love to retire and do nothing. Indeed, from the vantage point of a stressed-out, overworked employee, retirement sounds pretty good. Yet, not working can lead to laziness, boredom, and even an early death. Studies show that men who retire at age 65 have an average life expectancy of only two more years. On the other hand, men who continue to work part or full time once they reach 65 have a life expectancy of ten additional years. Work gives people something to live for. That's why many of the richest people in the world, such as Bill Gates and Ross Perot, continue to vigorously pursue goals in the material world. They could easily retire, but instead they choose to work hard doing what they feel passionate about.

The Antidote: Purposefulness

In studies designed to find out what really makes people happy, one thing almost always stands out as being the *most* important ingredient of lasting fulfillment. What do you think it is? I'll give you a hint—it's not being rich, beautiful, healthy, loved, talented, or intelligent. Rather, it's a trait or ability we all have equal access to: having a passionate sense of purpose. People who strongly believe in a cause or have goals that are truly important to them report that they are very fulfilled. People who lack a passionate sense of purpose or a deep sense of meaning in their lives report that they are much less happy. Even people who seem to have it all—wealth, looks, talent, love—but don't have a deep sense of purpose, are usually dissatisfied.

Since laziness leads to lethargy, and a strong sense of purpose leads to fulfillment, it's important to create a specific purpose you can always strive toward—no matter how much money you have. In the "money mission statement" from the first chapter, I had you focus on *why* you're deserving of the money you make, and how that money can improve your *own* life. Now, I suggest that you come up with a "personal mission statement" that describes what you'd most like to *contribute to the world*. By writing a sentence or two about your larger mission in life, it will help you overcome any tendency toward laziness. In addition, it will remind you of the importance of having a bigger purpose in life, and help guide you when making major life decisions.

I've come up with a simple formula for writing a personal mission statement. First, consider what you would want to do if you had $100 million but were required by law to work. What would you do for free—just because you feel that it's important work? *Who* would you want to help, and how? You might try making a list of causes that are important to you and see if there is a thread that ties them together. For example, if you listed that you'd like to save the whales, stop the killing of wolves, and protect the rain forests, your passionate sense of purpose might be to protect endangered species and the environment.

Next, decide what kind of person you'd like to BE. If you had no fear, in your heart what type of person would you most like to become? What would you like other people to say about you at your funeral? Whatever that is, it's important that you state it in your personal mission statement. It need not be perfect the first time you write it down. You can always tinker with it until it seems to really fit you. But any personal mission statement, even if it's not quite right, is better than having nothing at all to guide you.

Below I've listed several examples of personal mission statements. As you can see, they all start out with the words, "The purpose of my life is to be..." followed by a sentence describing what someone would like to contribute.

1. The purpose of my life is to be a daring explorer of human possibilities, inspiring and educating people to experience their own inner radiance through connection with Spirit.

2. The purpose of my life is to be a creative and loving parent, strengthening and influencing children to fully love themselves.

3. The purpose of my life is to be a powerful instrument
   of change, assisting and influencing businesses to seek
   environmental harmony on the planet.

4. The purpose of my life is to be a happy and humorous
   person, assisting sick people in achieving greater health
   and wholeness through the healing powers of play and
   humor.

In essence, the personal mission statement is a brief description of whom you'd like to be, whom you'd like to help, and *how*
you'd like to help. Previously, I mentioned that people who have
had an NDE report that they are asked the question, "How well
did you use the gifts you were given to contribute to people or the
world?" Your personal mission statement can help you pinpoint
exactly how you want to contribute, and remind you when you've
taken a wrong turn and fallen off your chosen course. As you
align yourself with your greater mission in life, you will avoid the
trap of laziness and connect with a way of feeling truly satisfied.
Take some time right now to write a rough draft of a personal
mission statement. Over time, feel free to modify it until it feels
just right. Once you have a statement that works for you, it can
act as a powerful reminder, motivating you to stay on target to
fulfill your deepest dreams.

Trap #5: Superiority

The fifth and final way in which people use money to impair
their spiritual unfoldment is when they begin to feel superior to
others. In the worst cases, money can be used to create an emotional wall of isolation. Safely hidden behind locked gates and
expensive cars, rich people can inadvertently stop the flow of
Spirit. The problem arises when money is used to create even

more separation than we normally feel. At its core, spiritual growth is a process of ending separation—whether it is overcoming separation from Spirit, other people, or one's own soul. When people use money to protect themselves from the hardships of life, the danger exists that it can also protect them from God's Grace.

Think about some rich people who you feel have not handled their wealth in a spiritual manner. What stands out? They probably seem arrogant, or at least not receptive to intimate contact. The desire to avoid our vulnerability is inherent in each of us, but increasing levels of wealth can make it easier to protect ourselves. It feels good to be a "big fish" in a little pond. We feel a certain type of safety and strength when we feel better than others. That's why so many people fall into this trap. On the other hand, feeling vulnerable, or like a little fish in a big pond, feels scary. It feels a bit out of control. Yet, the truth is that we *are* little fish in a big pond. Although we may hide that fact from ourselves, the effort it takes to do so separates us from Spirit.

The Antidote: Humility

While most people are put off by those who feel they're superior to others, we tend to be touched by people who are truly humble. Since I interviewed many of the most prominent spiritual leaders in the world for my *Bridges to Heaven* book (now renamed *The Experience of God)*, several people have asked me what it was like to be around them. If I had to state one or two traits that stood out in almost all the people I interviewed, I would say it was their humility and vulnerability. Despite their fame and accomplishments, they didn't feel or act superior. In fact, they were very aware of their shortcomings, and very honest about them. When we think of spiritually evolved souls, one person who stands out is Mahatma Gandhi—a man known for his humble ways. One of my favorite quotes from him is: "I have only three enemies. My favorite enemy, the one most easily influenced for the better is the British Empire. My second enemy, the Indian people, is far more difficult. But my most formidable opponent is a man named Mohandas K. Gandhi. With him I seem to have very little influence!"

A truly humble person touches us in a very deep way and helps to reduce the sense of separation we typically feel. So why is it so difficult to use money (and fame) to move toward humility—rather than superiority? Well, part of the problem is that it's easier to buy "protection" than ever before. We can buy bigger houses and a bigger security force, and with the aid of money, we can try to avoid all unpleasantness in life. In the short term, it even works, but in the long term it leaves us feeling empty.

How can wealth be used to create a deeper humility and connection with Spirit? Before we can answer that, we need to understand how true humility is born. I believe there are three things that help humility blossom in people: (1) a great purpose or challenge, (2) complete honesty, and (3) having a deep connection or yearning for God. Each of these three "avenues" can lead to humility, and having extra money *can* be helpful in pursuing each of these aims.

Let's first look at how a greater purpose can lead to humility. When we face a challenge much larger than we can possibly handle alone, it requires us to reach out. Whether we reach out to Spirit or to others, it expands the entity we are part of. As we identify with a larger entity, we become smaller in comparison. We are no longer fully in control. Under such conditions, humility is an indirect by-product. If we are interested in becoming part of a larger purpose, whether it is reducing starvation or expanding consciousness on the planet, having money can be helpful. Where our money goes, so go our thoughts and feelings. By using our money (as well as our time and energy) to pursue a large purpose, we "buy" our admission ticket to an entity much larger than our daily personal concerns. Humility is practically guaranteed to follow.

The second way to experience humility is to take a completely honest look at yourself. This may be hard to accomplish, but if you *can* do it, you're sure to feel humble. After all, our minds are almost completely out of control, and they never shut up. Selfishness, attachment, superiority, and laziness are constantly nipping at our souls. The only reason we don't feel humble more often is that we're experts at hiding our "dark side" from ourselves. Yet, if you can surround yourself with people, therapists, spiritual teachers, and/or workshops aimed at total honesty, you can become better acquainted with vulnerability and humility. In my own experience, I have found that such absolute honesty required outside help. Fortunately, I had the time and money to get the assistance I needed. Here again, the intelligent use of money can have important spiritual implications.

The third and final way to experience humility is to form a deep connection with God. Spirit is the ultimate larger entity. When we experience or become aware of the presence of God, we become nothing. Superiority can only exist if God is not part of our awareness. As soon as we even begin to taste of Spirit's energy, we feel humble. Although having money does not directly help us to experience God, it can make it more likely that a person will have time to think about such things. When people don't feel as if they have enough money, they usually spend *all* their time and energy pursuing it. Nothing is left over for spiritual pursuits. However, when people discover that making it big in the material world does not guarantee happiness, they often start to look for a deeper spiritual meaning and connection in their lives.

The art of money alchemy is an ongoing process. The moment we fail to use our awareness and connection with God to elevate how we deal with money, we begin to slide down into the money traps I've outlined in this chapter. Just as gravity is always working against our ability to soar through the air, the five money holes are continually pulling us away from our connection with Spirit. Fortunately, for each money hole, there is also a money helper—a way to use money to deepen our connection with Spirit. Our task is to use our awareness to sidestep the holes and grab hold of the lifelines that can further our spiritual development.

After reading about these money traps and noticing how difficult they are to overcome, you may be thinking that it's not worth the effort to try to make much money. I don't agree. Sure, you can live a nice "spiritual" life without making a lot of money or being very involved in the material world. Yet, I believe God calls us to experience living Spirit while *engaged* in the world—not separate from it. In the Bible it says that we are to "be in the world, but not of it." Just as a tree needs deep roots in the earth to grow high into the sky, I believe our "material roots" can help us grow stronger in our connection to Spirit. When we face and hopefully overcome the money traps I've outlined, the experience makes us strong, wise, and compassionate. We grow "spiritual muscles." From our spiritual wisdom and material success, we can give our very best to a hurting world.

REAL WEALTH REMINDERS

1. Increasing amounts of money can often help magnify a person's lower nature instead of bringing out their higher nature. Our job is to be aware of these money "traps" and, from our awareness, consciously steer ourselves toward loftier ways of handling our money.

2. The five most common money traps are: (1) feeling like there's never enough, (2) getting attached to your results, (3) becoming selfish, (4) getting lazy, and (5) feeling superior to others.

    The five corresponding antidotes for these traps are: (1) feeling grateful for what you have, (2) letting go, (3) being generous, (4) having a strong sense of purpose, and (5) feeling humble.

3. In order to maintain a spiritual way of handling money and work, it's helpful to write a personal mission statement in which you state whom you'd like to *be*, whom you'd like to *help*, and *how* you'd like to help. When you're aligned with your higher purpose, it's easy to avoid falling into money traps.

CHAPTER THREE

MONEY AND WORK AS SPIRITUAL TEACHERS

"Every man's task is his life preserver."
— Ralph Waldo Emerson

Throughout history, people have made use of teachers as a way of accelerating their spiritual growth. A teacher can point things out that interfere with spiritual progress and can also present challenges that aim to make a seeker stronger. In my own long association with a spiritual teacher, I found it invaluable to have someone who frequently challenged me, encouraged me, and taught me to be as impeccable as possible. Unfortunately, *good* spiritual teachers can be a bit hard to find nowadays. Yet, I believe there's a new kind of "teacher" whom people can learn from in this modern age. If the students are ready, their "teachers" can be the feedback they get from money and work.

A good teacher does not let you get away with any lies. In a similar way, money doesn't let you get away with any lies either. You have it—or you don't. A good teacher presents you with challenges to make you stronger and more capable. Money and work do the same thing. There are many parallels. So why is it that most people don't fully receive the lessons they could learn by looking at their money and work situations? In most cases, they blame forces beyond their control and don't recognize that they are fully responsible for what they create in their lives.

In my *Real Wealth* seminars, I walk among the participants and randomly ask several of them how much money they made last year. The room grows incredibly quiet. The tension in the air becomes so thick that many people actually stop breathing. After several people haltingly answer my question, I ask them to notice how they feel. I tell them to breathe again. Then I ask, "Why is it such a big deal how much money you or someone else made last year?" The answer is that we mistake our *own* worth as human beings for our *net* worth as human beings. The two are not really related. Yet, when we confuse the two, we become very defensive and uptight. It makes learning much more difficult.

As a psychotherapist, if I want to know the details of my clients' sex lives, I simply ask them. Most people are willing to be very frank about how their sex life is going—even if it's going poorly. Finding out about a person's financial situation is much more difficult. I've found that people often lie or give half-truths when I ask them about their finances. The fact that the amount of money we make is so emotionally charged interferes with our ability to be better at making it. Our "secretive" way of being around money also takes it out of the realm of Spirit. After all, Spirit and truth are intimately bound together. By being able to look directly at our feelings and inadequacies surrounding money, we can learn extremely valuable information about ourselves. In addition, as we overcome our defensiveness and receive the lessons offered to us, we can become more effective at *making* money.

Let's assume that everyone wants plenty of money to do what he or she deems important, and that everyone would also like to create this abundance by working at a truly rewarding job. That's the ideal. The reality, however, is that most people are making very little money doing a job they don't even care about. That's the problem. In order to go from "the problem" to the "ideal," a person has to be able to learn many lessons and overcome many challenges. It's just like an initiation process. With each challenge/initiation people face, they move closer to the ideal of creating abundance while doing what they love.

For many years, my partner, Helena, was a legal secretary. Although the money was adequate, she didn't find her job fulfilling. What she really wanted to do was be a massage therapist. Unfortunately, we live in Santa Barbara, California, where it seems that almost *everyone* is a licensed massage therapist. There are approximately 5,000 massage therapists in this town, in a population of only 100,000 people. Not exactly a good town to begin a massage practice! Nevertheless, I encouraged Helena to do what she loved, and if she were willing to face the challenge of working on her weaknesses, she could make a living giving massages. For years she resisted. She said there was too much competition. However, I pointed out that if she were willing to work on herself, she could overcome the many challenges she'd face while changing her career.

Finally, Helena couldn't stand her job as a legal secretary anymore. She quit and decided to do work for a temporary agency as she built up her massage practice. She was immediately forced to face her fear of not having enough money. She also came up against her resistance to promoting herself. The need for money was challenging her to face her fears, though. Fortunately, she was up to the test. Although she is basically a quiet person, she began walking into offices and offering people free ten-minute massages. Not only did this act of service make her and others feel good, it also led to acquiring some massage clients. As she received feedback about what worked and what didn't in her advertising and promotion, she secured more clients. Now, six months later, she has a strong massage practice and does not need to do any part-time work. She's ecstatic, and I'm very proud of her.

Helena is now able to make money doing what she loves

because she listened to the lessons money and work were trying to give her. She realized that it was only her fear and a lack of creative marketing that prevented her from doing what she really wanted to do. Once she faced her fears of failure, self-promotion, and not having enough money, the Universe rewarded her with a job she loves. Yet, as long as she wasn't facing her fears, she could not take the next step. That's the way the world works. When people have trouble in their work or money situation, there is always a lesson for them to receive. The question is, are they willing to receive it?

The Money Balloon

In my seminars, I tell people that they can move toward abundance and a job they truly love once they "fill the holes in their balloons." Even a tiny hole in a balloon makes it impossible to keep it inflated. Similarly, any weakness, fear, or erroneous belief we have about money will make it impossible to be full of abundance. Our personal "hole," or weakness, simply prevents us from moving forward. Our job is to figure out what our biggest hole is and fix it—so we can become more whole. As we work on our hole, or weakness, we become stronger. As we become more capable, we can begin to translate our newfound strength into more abundance and work we love.

Ram Dass, a former Harvard professor turned spiritual teacher, once shared with me the story of a man he met at a meditation retreat. Ram Dass asked the man what he did for a living, and the man said he was "vice president of industrial loans at a major bank." Ram Dass was surprised that such a man would be at a meditation retreat, so he asked him what his story was. It ends up that this man, whom we'll call Fred, was the vice president of loans at the same bank in the '70s. Yet, during this time he was miserable. It seemed like everyone back then was having a great time, and he was stuck in this lousy job that he hated. So Fred decided to quit his job and spend many years "following his bliss." He wrote poetry, did therapy, took workshops, meditated, and basically dropped out of society. Then, one day as he was walking through the streets of San Francisco, he stumbled upon his former boss—the president of the bank where he used to work. The bank president said, "It's quite a coincidence that I would see you today, because your old job just became available. You were the best vice president of industrial loans we ever had. Would you consider working for us again?"

Fred decided he'd give it a try. After many years of working on the "hole in his soul," he felt that it was time to see if things had changed. He shaved his beard, bought some suits, and sat at the same desk he had used a decade before. According to Ram Dass, Fred said that his "new" position felt completely different. He now loved his job. Fred described his office as a place where "I simply sit and hang out with divine beings all day long, and the vehicle for our hanging out is to talk about industrial loans." As Fred's story indicates, sometimes it is only an internal shift that's needed to feel more abundant or happier about one's work.

Finding and Filling Your Hole

In order to work on your faults, you first need to know what they are. Although this may seem easy, it is not. People tend to be blind to their own weaknesses. When I lived with 15 people in a spiritual commune, I got to see firsthand how ignorant people are about their own shortcomings. My teacher would occasionally put someone in our group on the "hot seat." He would compassionately, but honestly, detail many of the person's inadequacies while several of us watched. In almost every case, the people on the hot seat would defend themselves and elaborately explain that what my teacher was saying was totally inaccurate. Yet, from the vantage point of someone listening in, my teacher always seemed to be right on the mark—except when *I* was on the hot seat. When he detailed *my* faults, what he said was always full of misunderstandings, lies, and totally mistaken notions. It took me about a year before I realized that what was being said about me must actually be true—since he always seemed to be right about everyone else! I finally realized that I had managed to hide my weaknesses from only one person—myself.

There are several ways to become aware of your weaknesses without the aid of a spiritual teacher to point them out. Since there are holes in everyone's "balloon," what we really need to know is what prevents us from clearly seeing them. I believe there are four main "blinders" that keep us stuck. I call them blame, denial, distraction, and belief. I'll briefly discuss each of them.

First, there's blame. With this protective device, we manage to deceive ourselves into thinking that a problem is the fault of someone or something outside of ourselves. Helena originally believed that she couldn't make a living as a masseuse because there were already too many massage therapists in our town. Blame is hard to catch because there is usually an element of truth in what you're thinking. In Helena's case, it was true that the competition was fierce. Yet, it was *also* true that she was too afraid to market herself aggressively. In the case of Fred the banker, it was true that being a loan officer is not a wildly creative job. However, it was also true he was not able to see and enjoy the divinity of people while talking about loans. As Fred and Helena took responsibility for their weaknesses, they became stronger, more talented people. Soon, they were able to experience what they truly desired at work.

With respect to denial, the second defense mechanism, people simply ignore how they feel, or dispute that there might be anything better than what they currently have. Since you're voluntarily reading this book (I hope), you probably don't fit into this category. That's good. Denial is a tough defense to blast through.

Distraction is the third defense that keeps people from seeing themselves clearly. Whether the distraction is a result of TV, drugs, "busy"ness, or something else, it serves to keep people less aware of the problem at hand. For example, if a woman is unhappy with her work, she may put a lot of energy into other parts of her life to avoid the pain of a dissatisfying job. Distraction isn't always bad, though. We live in a challenging world, and sometimes we need to distract ourselves so we can feel okay. Yet, taken to an extreme, it keeps us stuck in behaviors and situations that are detrimental to our long-term growth and happiness.

The fourth and final defense is the problem of *belief.* Once we adopt a certain Belief System (B.S.), it can keep us stuck, unable to take the next step in our personal or professional growth. For example, an inventor might hold the false belief that if he could "build a better mousetrap, the world will beat a path" to his door. In truth, unless you market the mousetrap effectively, no one will know about it. A false belief can keep you busy expending energy in a direction that is ultimately useless. There are many erroneous beliefs that people hold about money, but one of the most common is the notion that they must choose between work they love and work that makes them a lot of money.

A financial advisor by the name of Srully Blotnick spent over ten years studying how people became millionaires. Mr. Blotnick found that the most common trait millionaires shared was that they did work they truly enjoyed! Because they enjoyed their work, they worked harder at it, stayed in it longer, and eventually rose to the top of their respective fields.

One false belief is all it takes to keep a person stuck. For example, if you held the false belief that you could only make a lot of money doing work you didn't enjoy—you'd be in trouble. If you took a job you didn't like just to make money, it could make your whole life miserable. To add insult to injury, it's unlikely you'd even make much money—because your lack of passion would probably interfere with your getting ahead in your career. Beware of the false beliefs that silently lurk within the confines of your own head. They can be dangerous.

Besides false beliefs about how best to make money, we can also hold detrimental beliefs about *ourselves* that greatly help or hinder our ability to create money and/or work we love. In my psychotherapy work, I've noticed that a lot of people don't feel worthy of creating work they enjoy, or they don't feel confident enough about their abilities. I've known artists who have incredible talent, but their own self-doubt prevents them from trying to make a living in the field. (In the next chapter, we'll talk about how to identify and neutralize dangerous beliefs you may have picked up as a child.)

I'm often asked in my seminars, "How can we know what the hole in our money balloon is when the defenses of blame, denial, distraction, and belief serve to hide this information from ourselves?" I wish there was an easy answer. It can be difficult to know exactly what we most need to work on in order to become stronger. Yet, I do have a few helpful hints. First, you can ask people you trust and know well to tell you what *they* think you need to work on. It can be painful to hear the truth, but it can save you a lot of pain in the long run.

About a year ago, a good friend of mine asked me, "Would you like to know what I think is keeping you from greater success?" It was an offer I couldn't refuse. My friend was brutally honest. He said, "Jonathan, you dress like you're 14 years old. Almost everything you wear announces that you're not a professional. You dress like a little kid. You'll never get to the next level of your career dressed like that." Ouch. What made his words sting even more was that I knew they were true. We made a deal that he'd go to my house and throw out everything he thought made me look like a kid. By the time he was done, I was left with a few pieces of underwear. In desperation, I took 20 percent of the clothes back from the "Goodwill pile." Yet, in order to have something to wear for more than three days, I had to go shopping.

My friend and I went to Nordstrom's together, and I bought a whole new wardrobe. Since investing in these new clothes a year ago, my income has risen about 30 percent. Coincidence? I don't think so. When we fill the holes in our money balloon, magic happens.

Although brutal self-honesty can be difficult to come by, it is not impossible. If you examine your history at work and your experiences with money, you may be able to guess what your deficiencies are. I have found three questions to be of particular help in getting people to pinpoint the areas they need to work on. The first question is "What have I historically avoided or found difficult in the world of money and/or work? There's a good chance that what you've avoided has prevented you from experiencing greater freedom with your career and money. In my own case, I had always avoided wearing business clothes. With my T-shirts and jeans, I rebelliously felt superior to those who had succumbed to wearing suits and ties. I still don't *like* wearing business clothes. Yet, when a situation calls for professional attire, I've learned that wearing a suit helps me make more of an impact on the people I'm dealing with. It's natural that, as I've been willing to grow and learn my lessons, I've been rewarded with more money.

A second question that can offer you insight into your shortcomings is, "If I had no fear, how would I act differently?" Frequently, our fears keep us from taking the actions that would lead us to career and monetary success. There are many types of fear. Common ones include the fear of rejection, the fear of failure, anxiety about being broke, and the fear that you're not good enough at a particular skill. If you make a list of all the ways you would behave differently if you had no fear, you'll probably become aware of several holes in your money balloon. Then, all you need do is decide which one is the biggest or most limiting, and begin to work on that.

There is a third and final question to help you pinpoint deficiencies that might be limiting your success. You can use this question anytime a situation arises that does not go as well as you'd like. Simply ask yourself, "What could this situation possibly be showing me about myself?" Like a good teacher, this question helps you release blame and take responsibility for whatever is happening. To be even more precise at taking responsibility, you might ask yourself, "What shortcomings in me might have led to this situation, and how can I work on them?" These questions are indeed challenging, but they are an efficient way of becoming aware of the holes in your balloon.

I had a client named Frank who, despite being an excellent carpenter, was making very little money. He hardly ever received referrals, and even when he had work, he consistently made his bids for jobs too low to make a profit. At first, Frank blamed his clients for his problems. In therapy, I pointed out to Frank that blaming others was not going to put more money in his pocket. I asked Frank the question, "What deficiencies in you may have led to this situation?" From this question, Frank was able to see two important things about himself. First, he realized that he didn't get referrals because he was too embarrassed to ask for them. Simply put, he was afraid of being rejected. Second, Frank often left a job feeling angry with his customers because the bid he had given them was too low in the first place. His annoyed attitude made it even more unlikely he'd get referrals.

By answering the questions, "What shortcomings in me have led to this situation, and how can I work on them?" he realized that his fear of rejection was compelling him to make his bids very low, as well as keeping him from asking for referrals. He vowed to make his bids for jobs 20 percent higher, and to ask each of his customers for at least one referral. It was daunting for Frank to do this, but it paid off. He soon found that, despite the fact he didn't always get the jobs he bid for, he ended up making more money than before. Because he was now making additional money on each of his jobs, he ended up treating his customers better. By the time he asked them for referrals, most were happy to recommend him to others. Within two months, Frank had increased his income by a substantial amount. In addition, his customers were more satisfied because his work and attitude were better.

Even the greatest spiritual teacher can't help someone who doesn't want to learn. On the other hand, someone who is eager to soak up information can be taught by *any* situation or person. There's an ancient Zen story of a monk who became enlightened just by watching the behavior of his own dog. Ultimately, we can each decide to learn from our experiences, or use various defenses to hide our faults from ourselves. If we really are receptive, the lessons stemming from our current money and work situations can greatly accelerate our personal, spiritual, and career growth. I encourage you to ask your friends and yourself about the holes in your balloon. As you work on your deficiencies, you'll become stronger, more prosperous, and more capable of giving to a world in need of your help.

REAL WEALTH REMINDERS

1. Our money and work history can offer us clues that point to our shortcomings. As we overcome our defensiveness and receive the lessons offered to us, we can become more effective at making money and enjoying our work.

2. We all have "holes" in our "money balloons." Our job is to know what the biggest holes are and fix them. Unfortunately, the defenses of denial, blame, distraction, and false belief can serve to hide our inadequacies from ourselves.

3. To know exactly what the biggest holes in your money balloon are, ask a trusted friend. Or, when money/work problems arise, ask yourself the following question: "What shortcomings in me might have led to this situation, and how can I work on them?"

CHAPTER FOUR

YOUR UNIQUE MONEY AND WORK PROFILE

*"There is a gigantic difference between earning
a great deal of money and being rich."*
— Marlene Dietrich

Every person in the world has a distinctive fingerprint and DNA blueprint. I believe we also have a unique "money/work print" as well. From our genes and from the environment we were born into, we develop beliefs, challenges, and abilities that are specific to ourselves. The task we are given is to listen to our particular path and translate it into a method of making money that is both enjoyable and valuable to others. In the last chapter, I talked about the need to receive the lessons that money and work are trying to give you. Being open to "hearing" the lessons is more than half the battle. Yet, once you become more aware of your particular challenges, what do you do with them? First, I'll answer that question, then I'll discuss how to make use of the distinctive strengths you've been given.

Your Specific Challenges

You grew up in a family that instilled very precise ideas and messages about money and work in you. If you're like most people, many of these messages were negative or highly restrictive. In chapter 1, I discussed a way to reprogram your old associations about money and begin connecting it to what you really value. Yet, sometimes it can be helpful to explore specific messages you received as a child, and like a surgeon, remove cancerous thoughts that may be especially damaging. For example, I once worked with a client named Cheryl who, as a child, repeatedly heard the message, "We can't afford it until Grandma dies." After a while, Cheryl remembers secretly hoping that Grandma would die so she could finally get some of the things she wanted. Well, Grandma *did* finally die, and Cheryl felt extremely guilty. By the time Cheryl was an adult, she created the thought that having money resulted in other people's deaths or misfortunes. No wonder she never had much money!

What negative messages did you receive about money and work when you were growing up? Were there certain phrases you remember your parents repeatedly saying, such as: "Money doesn't grow on trees" or "I hate going to work in the morning"? Were there messages you picked up from your parents as a result of the way they handled money or how they argued about it with each other? Most likely, early childhood messages are still buried somewhere in your subconscious, and they can influence your behavior in ways you aren't even aware of.

A simple way to get in touch with negative thoughts about money and work that you picked up as a child is to write down the words, "I deserve wealth and fulfillment." Then, simply keep repeating these words and write down any contrary thoughts or images that pop up. From the money seminars I lead, I've learned that the following phrases and messages were common to many homes. Do any of them seem familiar to you?

1. We can't afford that! We're not rich.
2. Work was a bitch today (or some version of that).
3. The boss has been on my back all week.
4. Look at what snobs those (rich) people are.
5. I work my tail off to put a roof over your head.
6. Money is to be saved, not enjoyed.
7. Too much money is the devil's curse.
8. You work to make a living, not because you like your job.
9. Making money is hard work that leaves a person drained and irritable.
10. You're lucky to have anything because there are people who have nothing.

When you become aware of a specific negative phrase or message that you picked up as a child, it's important to know how to neutralize its impact on you. A simple way to reprogram limiting childhood messages is to come up with a single phrase or affirmation that counters the message you received while growing up. For instance, if you got the message that "money is to be saved, not enjoyed," then you'd want to come up with a single sentence that somehow counters or transforms that limiting idea. You might affirm something like, "Money is to be invested in my pleasure and my future."

When creating a new phrase, it's helpful if the sentence succinctly expresses what you want your new belief to be. It should feel good to you. When you have come up with a new phrase that counters a limiting belief from your past, you can practice saying or singing it to yourself over and over again. After a while, like a computer, your subconscious will update your old "program" and "install" the new message you're giving it.

Affirmations are simply brief statements of beliefs that somehow inspire you, or help you past your old, limiting conditioning. For example, the affirmation I use is: "An abundance of money flows effortlessly into my life." This statement helps me counteract the conditioning I received as a child that said: "It takes a lot of work at an unenjoyable job to make money." Below is a list of affirmations about money that you might find helpful:

1. The more wealth I receive, the more love I can give.
2. God has given me talents to make money so I can benefit others and myself.
3. As I express my full self in the world, I am rewarded with material abundance.
4. I enjoy the challenge of gaining financial mastery.
5. As I give people my very best, I receive wealth, love, and freedom.

If one of these affirmations touches you in some way, use it. Or, if you prefer, create a phrase that meets your unique needs. Affirmations can be especially effective if combined with intense mental pictures, sounds, and feelings. For instance, by repeating an affirmation while imagining your particular monetary dream, you can build an emotional momentum that can plow through any obstacles.

In the case of my client, Cheryl, she realized that she had installed the belief in her mind that "the money I receive is blood money." Not exactly an inspiring belief to hold. I asked her, "What belief would you *like* to have about the money you receive?" She said she'd like to believe that the money she receives is a gift from God to help her become a better person. I suggested she sing to herself many times a day, "God's gift to thee—to help me be free—is the money that is given to me." I know it sounds corny, but the subconscious mind likes corny rhymes and cute phrases. That's why we hear so many jingles on TV and in radio commercials. Once Cheryl starting singing this phrase, she found it hard to get it out of her head. Within a few days, she could feel a definite change in her reaction to receiving money. Within a few months, she was making more money than she had ever made!

Although reprogramming the specific limiting messages you picked up as a child takes some work, it can reap large rewards. Many of my clients have told me that they didn't realize how burdensome their old beliefs were until they let go of them. One client described the change in this way: "I used to go to work with what felt like a Greyhound bus on my shoulders. I'd come home every day feeling defeated. After a week of singing my new phrase, I feel like I'm going to work with a guardian angel on my shoulder. When I return home, I still have energy."

It's never too late to change what's between your ears.

The Cosmic Hot and Cold Game

Remember the hot and cold game you used to play as a child? Someone would hide an object, such as a dollar, and you would try to find it. Whenever you got closer to where it was hidden, you'd be told that you were getting "warmer." When you wandered farther from the dollar's hiding place, you'd be informed you were getting "colder." Eventually, you'd get "red hot" and would find the hidden object.

I believe God is really playing the hot and cold game with each of us. We're all trying to find the perfect job for us—work that is both highly enjoyable and profitable. God—or the Universe—is continually sending us messages with respect to whether we're getting nearer or farther from this goal. There are two ways in which such messages are communicated. First, when we enjoy our work or find it particularly rewarding, that's a message that we're getting "warmer." Such an internal experience means that we're doing something right. When we feel that our work is unrewarding or boring, that means we're getting cooler. It's time to reevaluate the direction in which we're going.

The second way we receive messages about how we're doing is by the external feedback we get. If you invent a widget and someone offers you a lot of money for it, that's a good indication that you're on the right path. On the other hand, if you never sell what you create, that can be an indication that there's something not quite right. By listening to the inner and outer messages the Universe sends your way, you can soon learn to steer yourself to the treasure that awaits you—work you enjoy and find profitable.

When I began my career, I used a different technique for trying to figure out what I should do. I thought that if I meditated enough, God would speak to me in a booming voice and tell me exactly what avenue I was supposed to pursue. I call this the "Moses model" for finding your life's work. Many spiritually inclined people believe that God will one day speak to them in a distinct manner and say, "You need to go this way!" After all, that's what He did with Moses, so why not with you and me? Actually, God didn't do that with Moses. Moses had to stumble along for many years on his own before he received direct and clear guidance from Spirit. I believe that we have to do the same thing. Only after a long time of listening to the hot and cold feedback we get from the Universe does it become clear what God wants us to do.

After many years of discerning when I've been warmer or cooler, it *has* become clear what my unique purpose is. Yet, I have traveled an often-crooked line toward my goal of knowing my life's work. I have had to endure dozens of messages that, in effect, said, "You're freezing." Fortunately, like a "connect the dots" drawing that's been filled in, the picture of what my purpose is has become strikingly clear. Each time I acted and got the message I was off course, I became wiser. I learned perseverance and compassion. Each time I acted and got the feedback I was *on* course, I became wealthier and more able to contribute to others. Through this feedback process, God teaches us to be strong, flexible, persistent, and humble.

Some people are secretly angry with God for not being directly guided to what they should do. They don't want to take action when they're uncertain, or make a few wrong turns along the way. Yet, I believe *we need* to go through the "hot and cold process" in order to become stronger, more spiritual people. It's only through overcoming difficulties that we become spiritually strong, just as it is only through lifting weights that we become physically powerful. In my own life, I have seen how going through this process has made me smarter, more capable, and better able to handle the many challenges of the material world.

I would like to say that I've learned my lessons and am now done with the universal hot and cold game. Such is not the case. When my second book came out, *The Little Book of Big Questions,* I intuitively felt that I didn't need to promote it. Then my linear mind kicked in and told me I had to promote it or no one would ever hear about it. Over several weeks I managed to call over 300 radio stations and newspapers about my book—hating every minute of it. To my amazement, not a single person responded. The Universe was practically screaming at me, "You're now freezing." Realizing I was off course, I went to a friend for guidance. She suggested that I read the book again and get in touch with how valuable it is. She also suggested that I not try to promote it, but instead ask in meditation if there was any fun way I might let others know about the book.

While in meditation, I got the idea that, on Christmas Day, families could use the questions in my book as a way to talk about spiritual topics and keep the spirit of Christmas alive. I made a single call to CNN about this idea, and they loved it. They interviewed me for a full 15 minutes, and it went extremely well. Then, the producers of *Oprah* saw this interview and decided to base an entire show on the questions in my book. With a single well-placed call and idea, my book now soared onto the bestseller list. Working in cahoots with Spirit is a lot more fun and rewarding than trying to push through our own agenda.

As spiritual beings, we have a subtle balance to maintain. One part of our task is to take a lot of action, learning from the feedback we receive—as in the hot and cold game. The other part of our task is to take action inspired from a deeper place within ourselves. In the above example, I took a lot of action, but it wasn't in line with my intuition. Therefore, the results were not good. Finding the right balance of intuition and action is an ongoing process. Yet, there are signs indicating when you've veered too far toward either side.

A sign that you're living by the "Moses model"—meaning you're not taking enough action—is that nothing ever gets accomplished. Taking action and failing is better than never taking any action at all. We've all known people who have grandiose visions of what they'd like to create, but never seem to do anything but dream. It's a shame because their ideas may be great, but they lack the "strength" to manifest their dreams. People like this need to dive into learning by action, make a few wrong turns, and become wiser from their efforts.

On the other side of the fence are people who are always taking action but who never listen to what their soul is saying. They get a lot done, and sometimes even rise to the top of their industry. Unfortunately, their feeling of dissatisfaction is evidence that they are off course. Taking action predicated only on the desire for personal profit is damaging to one's soul, one's relationship with other people, and even damaging to the planet. It is only when we strike the right balance of taking massive action—guided by God's will as best we can discern—that we can accomplish our dreams and have a good time doing it.

Cashing in Your Gifts

In business and marketing, there is an important concept referred to by the term *unique selling proposition,* or U.S.P. In essence, it refers to the aspect of your product or service that is different from your competitor's. By knowing your unique selling proposition, it's possible to market your product or service much more effectively. I have taken the idea of U.S.P. and altered it to come up with the term *unique skills and abilities,* or U.S.A. By knowing what skills and abilities are unique to you, you can receive valuable clues as to what kind of work would be most satisfying and profitable.

I had a client named Michelle who came into my office suffering from depression. She had a job as a receptionist but was profoundly bored. I realized that one reason for her depression was the fact that she hadn't tapped into her unique skills or abilities. I asked her, "What would your friends say you're particularly good at?" She mentioned how her friends often make fun of how organized she was, and how clean she keeps her apartment. Then I asked her, "Do you like organizing and cleaning?" Michelle practically lit up when she said how she enjoys getting projects organized and completed. She gave me a few examples of parties she had created for friends, projects she had done for charities, and systems she had created to get more accomplished in her life.

Michelle, like everyone, had unique abilities. Unfortunately, she wasn't using them in her current job. Therefore, she felt bored and unfulfilled. I suggested that she find a job where she had more responsibility and could use her formidable organizing and planning skills. She was too afraid to quit her current job without knowing what she would find. After some discussion, we agreed that she could start a little business in her spare time as a party planner. She had some business cards made up and put an ad in the paper. It was two months before she got her first call to organize a party. Yet, she was so good at what she did that, within six months, she had more jobs than she could handle. Therefore, she quit her job as a receptionist and became a party and event planner full time. A by-product of her change of jobs was the fact that her depression mysteriously disappeared. Using your U.S.A. can have distinct advantages.

If you would like to follow in Michelle's footsteps, there are three important steps to take to cash in on your unique skills and abilities. First, find out the answer to the first question that I asked Michelle: What would your friends say you're good at? If possible, ask several of your friends this question. You may be surprised at their answers. It's also helpful to ask *yourself* this question, and along with your friend's responses, make a list of the answers you receive. Next, ask yourself, "What do I like to do?" Once again, making a list is beneficial. Finally, look at what's on your lists and ask yourself, "How can I use these skills and things I enjoy to make more money?" You may even want to ask this question in meditation and wait for an answer that feels right. The answer may not come right away. Yet, as it says in the Bible, "Ask and it shall be given unto you." If you focus on this question long enough, an exemplary answer will eventually become clear to you.

Once you have an indication of how you can use your U.S.A. to make more money, begin the implementation process. With each action you take, listen for the "hot and cold" feedback you receive. Over time, you'll be guided toward work that you enjoy and find profitable. You don't need to know all the answers (the Moses model) to begin your journey of wealth. Armed with your unique skills and abilities and a way of learning from the feedback you receive, you can follow the road that leads to riches—both internally and externally.

REAL WEALTH REMINDERS

1. Being aware of your unique gifts and obstacles to creating wealth can be helpful in turning them into moneymaking and personal growth opportunities. For example, by being cognizant of your negative childhood programming surrounding money, you can create an appropriate affirmation to neutralize its impact.

2. To know what you're being "guided" to do, listen for the external and internal feedback you receive from the Universe. When you enjoy something, it feels right to you, or it gets great results, that probably means you're getting "warmer." When something feels wrong, meaningless, or gets poor results, that most likely means you're getting "cooler."

3. By knowing what you're good at and what you like to do, you can often translate such skills and abilities into an enjoyable way to make money.

PART TWO

From Soul to Goal

CHAPTER FIVE

THE SOUL AT WORK

"Where the whole man is involved, there is no work."
— Marshall McLuhan

The soul is something that is hard to define. Webster's dictionary defines it as "the spiritual principle embodied in human beings." Whatever the soul is, there is general agreement that it imbues human beings with a certain goodness that is a reflection of a higher power. On the other hand, the words *business* or *work* do not necessarily connote a sense of goodness. In fact, the opposite is often true. People sometimes even use the term *did his business* to refer to a dog relieving itself or a child soiling his or her diaper. To use the phrase *a soulful business* sounds like an oxymoron to many people. Yet, there are many "characteristics" of the soul that can actually be extremely valuable in the work environment. By tapping into these soul traits, people can experience more internal and external success while pursuing their careers.

In this chapter, I'm going to discuss five characteristics of the soul. I'll explore how to delve more deeply into each of these soul traits, and how they can be utilized in the work environment.

The five aspects of soul that I've chosen are passion, creativity, selfless service, equanimity, and humility. There are many other characteristics of the soul that could have been used, but these five were chosen because they each have profound implications for how we approach our careers. By exploring how these five specific spiritual traits can impact your work environment, I hope you'll come to a greater understanding of how to unleash the power of your soul at work.

Characteristic #1: Pursuing Your Passion

In chapter 3, I mentioned how Srully Blotnick, after ten years of research, came to an unexpected conclusion about who became rich. Mr. Blotnick had expected to find that most people become millionaires through real estate or high-paying corporate jobs. Yet, his research indicated otherwise. After poring over mounds of data, Mr. Blotnick concluded that the people who got rich were those who reported that they absolutely loved what they did. No matter what line of work people were in, if they possessed a passion for their work, they tended to rise to the top of their field—where the big bucks existed. If you really enjoy what you do for money, then you don't ever have to *work* for a living.

In chapter 2, under the "purposefulness" subheading, I discussed how to write a personal mission statement that would help clarify what your passionate sense of purpose is. Once you have a sense of what that might be, the next step is to figure out how to make money by pursuing your passion—if you aren't already doing so. A good question to ask your intuition or Spirit is, "How can I make money doing what I love and feel passionate about?" Besides your intuition, you can ask this question to your friends, colleagues, and people who are already making money in the field you're interested in. Why reinvent the wheel? If you know of someone who makes a living in the area you'd like to go into, give him or her a call. Explain your situation and ask for advice. I've done this many times myself and have found people to be of enormous help and very generous with their time.

Perhaps you already know what your passion is, but you're too afraid to let go of your old source of income to fully pursue it. If you plan carefully, you can make a gradual transition from your old job to a new career. Nowadays, people change jobs an average of seven times over the course of their lives. It's common to work at one job while preparing academically or financially for another. By constructing a clear-cut plan on paper (as you'll be guided to do in chapter 7), you can avoid any insecurity that may arise when you think about changing your source of income.

Characteristic #2: Selfless Service

Selfless service has been part of almost every spiritual tradition since time began. Despite its position of respect in the spiritual traditions, the practice of selfless service has not caught fire in the business world, however. In fact, just the opposite is true. Even good service, much less selfless service, is a rare commodity in America. People tend to do as little as they feel they can get away with. The result of this way of doing business is a general cynicism and lack of loyalty on the customer's part. By learning and practicing the art of selfless service in business, it's possible to enjoy your job more, grow spiritually, and create more business than you ever thought possible.

When my girlfriend, Helena, began marketing herself as a massage therapist, she would walk into offices and offer people a free ten-minute massage. Her primary motive was selfless service. She found that she enjoyed making people feel good, and giving people free massages was her small way of giving back to the community. If, after the massage, someone asked her for her card, she'd give it—but with no sense of trying to "sell" them anything. Her purity of motivation paid off. Many people asked her for her card because they sensed her genuine concern for their well-being. Without delivering any kind of sales pitch, Helena soon had a full-time massage therapy practice.

I define selfless service as the art of providing people with more than they could possibly expect—just for the joy of it. When we think in terms of how we can give people our best, it can add to our own enjoyment of work. In seminars, I used to give my best only on the rare occasion when there was a large crowd. Yet, I discovered that when I gave 100 percent all of the time, I enjoyed myself more, my audience enjoyed it immensely, and soon there were larger crowds to give my best to!

In my dealings with various businesses, I am often amazed by the generally uncaring and inconsiderate demeanor of their employees. Their attitude seems to be, "I was having a perfectly fine time sitting around, and then this customer comes in and expects me to help him—can you *believe* that?" In an effort to cut costs, many businesses have laid off employees—with the result being that there is even *less* service. Yet, I've noticed that many people are willing to pay more money to have good service. I find myself patronizing businesses that make a little extra effort to do things right—despite the fact that they may charge a bit more. At the companies where I've given lectures, there seems to be a lot of agreement that excellent service pays for itself over time. The reason is simple: Superior service leads to repeat customers and referrals, and repeat customers and referrals are the easiest and most effective way to build a business.

If excellent service leads to a better bottom line, why doesn't everyone jump on the bandwagon? Two reasons. First, giving good service initially costs more. It requires more motivated or higher-caliber employees, or simply more workers to do a given job. The bottom-line benefit of providing outstanding service takes some time (as customers come back or as referrals are made). Unfortunately, businesses nowadays tend to think about their quarterly bottom line, rather than their long-term prospects. The second reason great service is rare is that it initially takes more work, and it's hard to find or train people to put out such effort. Yet, it's energy well spent. A company that can develop a reputation for consistently providing excellent customer service, such as the Nordstrom department store chain, can cash that reputation into their bank account.

We've talked about the financial benefits of selfless or truly excellent service, but what about the spiritual benefits? Once again, most people don't practice it because the initial payoff seems small, but its long-term payoff is huge. There's a price people pay when they go to work and have the attitude, "What's in it for me?" Such thinking breeds cynicism, jealousy, a lack of cooperation, lessened productivity, and apathy. Imagine how different work would feel if you saw each customer you served or each project you worked on as a way of serving God? Imagine how different that might feel!

When the late Mother Teresa was asked how she could do her work, her answer was, "I see my beloved Christ in all His distressing disguises. How can I not serve people?" If we can learn to see the pain in the people we do business with, it can help us want to serve them from our hearts, rather than just from our desire for money.

A question I often ask myself when I'm helping a client in psychotherapy is "If I were in their shoes, how would I like to be treated?" I also ask, "How can I give them even more value than they could possibly expect?" Asking these two questions places my focus on *their* needs, rather than mine. It also makes me feel excited about truly giving them my best. I love it when people say that they received a lot more than they expected. Giving people my best makes my clients feel good—but it also makes *me* feel good.

A chiropractor friend of mine saw that after many years of running a successful practice, his reason for helping people had changed. Originally, he became a chiropractor to help people, but success and the desire for money had slowly preempted these altruistic feelings. To get back to his original, pure motivation, he took out a big ad in the local paper that read: "Chiropractor offers free adjustments for all those in need." The ad went on to explain *why* he would be offering free adjustments to anyone who needed them (one day a week). Hundreds of desperate people showed up for his free services. As people in pain profusely thanked him for changing their lives, my friend once again got in touch with his desire to serve people. Although he worried about the effect this practice might have on his paying clients, it actually increased his business. People felt good about seeing a chiropractor who was willing to go the extra mile to help those who could not pay.

Ram Dass once told me how he explained the concept of giving people more than they could possibly expect to his dad, a prominent businessman. His father had asked him why he gave so much to people for so little money. Ram Dass said, "Remember when Uncle Harry needed your services and you didn't charge him?" Ram Dass's father answered, "Well, of course I didn't charge him—he's your Uncle Harry." Ram Dass said, "Well, that's my problem. Everyone I serve feels like my Uncle Harry."

Indeed, we are all connected. What goes around, comes around. Giving people your best and serving them as if they were your Uncle Harry makes good business sense—while feeding your soul.

Characteristic #3: Creativity

Creativity is a third way to translate the power of the divine into success in the marketplace. From Einstein's theory of relativity to Edison's invention of the phonograph, tapping into creative ideas has made many people rich and driven technology forward. In this day and age of rapid change, people who can tap into the creative energy of their souls are at a major advantage over those who follow the crowd.

It used to be that only certain materials were valuable, and the people who could monopolize those materials became rich. Things are quickly changing. Now there is a marketplace of creative ideas, and many people become wealthy simply by coming up with a novel way of doing something. For example, computer software is basically human ingenuity and creativity—the actual disk costs next to nothing. The same is true for computer chips, which are now some of the most valuable commodities on earth—even bringing in more money than oil. Yet, a computer chip is worthless in and of itself—it is only made of sand. It is human ingenuity and creativity that has allowed us to turn dirt (sand) into such a precious resource!

Despite the enormous value of creativity in the marketplace, it is not commonly taught or discussed in business schools, and not overtly encouraged in corporations. Many business people are afraid of their creative urges, so they suppress them in order to maintain a feeling of security and safety. What we need to recognize is that by systematically tapping into our creative ideas and impulses, it's possible to bring our deeper self, our soul, into our work.

While this is not a book on how to tap into one's creativity, I'd like to suggest a few guidelines that can be of enormous help. Perhaps the most important step is to truly appreciate one's own creative energy. Most people value watching TV, keeping busy, or just about anything else over attending to their creative impulses. Like a physical muscle that goes unused, their creative muscles soon atrophy.

When I was 16 years old, ideas for song lyrics started running through my head. When this happened, I felt as if Grace was descending on me and that it was important to write down what I was receiving. In fact, I made a vow that whenever I felt the flow of creative ideas, I would stop what I was doing and write them down. On numerous occasions, my vow has been tested—such as the time a song lyric ran through my head while taking my graduate exams. Yet, I've kept my promise. Because I've made listening to my creative urges a priority, they seem to keep on coming. Over the last 20 years, I've made most of my income from listening to and following through on these creative and intuitive impulses.

Besides valuing your creative urges, it's also helpful to know what blocks you from being open to creativity and what helps you be receptive to it. There are numerous books that can be of help in this regard, such as *A Whack on the Side of the Head,* by Roger Von Oech; *Six Thinking Hats,* by Edward DeBono; and *The Well of Creativity,* by Julia Cameron and other contributors. I have found that most people already know what fosters creativity in them. All you need to do is ask yourself, "What could I do to be more open to creativity in my work?" For myself, I have found that frequent short vacations, daily meditation, a sense of humor, and the ability to play with ideas have all been of enormous help in keeping creative energies flowing.

It is also important to know what blocks you from allowing creative energy to be a consistent source of inspiration in your life. Sometimes one faulty belief or negative thought can interfere with the flow of creative juices. Many people are afraid they'll look stupid if they manifest these impulses. Because they're not willing to be vulnerable in this way, they subconsciously block the creativity that Spirit is sending them. If you feel you sometimes do this, try unleashing your creative ideas without showing the result to anyone. Over time, you may decide that some of your impulses are worth sharing. Who knows, maybe a great novel or the next super widget is waiting to manifest through you—and all you need to do is give yourself permission to allow these creative urges to come through.

Characteristic #4: Equanimity

Equanimity is the ability to experience peace of mind even under difficult conditions. If you're going to do business and make money, it's likely that you'll experience some degree of stress. Yet, a spiritual approach to money means that you try to maintain a connection to peace while engaged in the world. The old adage is: "Be *in* the world, but not *of* it." Most people would agree that maintaining peace while involved in the world is a noble goal, but they've never stopped to consider how it may also improve their bottom line. While talking to successful business people, I've noticed that many of them have emphasized the need to avoid acting from their emotions. Whatever a person does for a living, acting from emotions can be very costly.

In order to experience equanimity in the midst of modern-day life and money, many things are needed. First, a person needs a connection to a bigger picture. On the daily roller coaster ride of business pursuits, it's easy to get so caught up in the moment that all sense of peace and perspective is lost. From the stress that results from such a ride, poor decisions are often made, and unfortunate behaviors can result. Yet, when a person can sense the greatness of their soul, daily troubles shrink in comparison. People who teach stress reduction often say, "Don't sweat the small stuff, and remember, it's *all* small stuff."

Imagine that you have a black dot the size of a quarter on the page in front of you. If your eyeball were right on top of that black dot, all you would see is black. A person in such a position would rightfully state, "I see nothing but a big black void, devoid of any color. That's all there is out here—total darkness." Equanimity is the art of being able to back away from the page and see that the black dot is actually quite small in comparison to everything else. From a yard away, a quarter-size dot is no big deal; from across the room, it's hardly noticeable.

There are numerous ways to keep a sense of perspective

while participating in daily life. Some have already been mentioned in this book. Practices such as meditation, spending time in nature, reading from holy books, or listening to certain music can all be of help in regaining our perspective when it's been lost. The important thing is to find a way that works for you that is quick, effective, and *can be done while at your office*. In my own case, I have found that certain songs that really touch me in a profound way can help me quickly tap into the equanimity of my soul. In fact, I've made four cassette tapes that are filled with all my favorite songs. Whenever I feel out of whack, I put a tape in my Walkman and take a five-minute vacation from the drama of daily life. Then, I read a statement that's printed next to my desk. It says, "The sun is one of a billion stars in the Milky Way galaxy. There are over a billion galaxies in the known Universe, each with about a billion stars. Don't sweat the small stuff...." That usually helps.

In order to experience equanimity in relation to work and money, I've found another skill particularly useful. I call it the ability to see the opportunity in adversity. If you truly knew that the "bad things" that happened to you were really great gifts in disguise, you would not become so worried. You would peacefully and curiously wait for the Grace to appear. Of course, we all intellectually know that positive things can result from problems, but it's a major challenge to experience peace of mind while such difficulties are hitting you in the face.

A few years back, I was giving a lecture on how positive results can arise from seemingly disturbing problems. During the class break, a student I knew approached me and said he had something for me in his car. I followed him and waited while he looked for "it." As he searched, I became increasingly annoyed because I was taking too much time from class. Every time I was about to head back, he'd say, "Wait! I think I found it." It was not to be. Finally, I insisted on returning to class. As I entered the room, about 100 people yelled, "Surprise!" It was the day after my birthday, and most of my friends had come to throw me a party.

What was humbling about this experience was the fact that I had just been talking about seeing what is positive in adversity but had totally missed the opportunity when it happened. I realized that in order to feel peace during difficult times, a very simple and precise technique was needed. The idea alone is not enough to help when adversity strikes. Therefore, I've tried various methods that I thought would help. Most have failed miserably, but one method has withstood the test of time and challenge. Whenever a problem arises, I simply ask myself, *"What could potentially be good about this?"* Then, even if I don't believe what I'm saying initially, I come up with at least two positive outcomes relating to the troubling situation. If nothing else, when difficulties arise in my life, they can always help me develop inner traits such as compassion, patience, humility, and faith.

The question, "What could potentially be good about this?" is a great aid to gaining equanimity in life. Besides the fact that it takes your mind off the negative aspects of the situation at hand, it can help you see potential opportunities that were invisible to you before. Most growth, whether it is personal or professional, comes from facing challenges and turning them into opportunities. If you can sincerely ask yourself the above question when you're upset or stressed, you can quickly find your way back to a feeling of equanimity.

Characteristic #5: Humility

Humility is the fifth and final soul trait that can make a world of difference at work. Humility sometimes gets a bum rap because it sounds like humiliation. Whereas no one likes to feel humiliated, true humility feels wonderful—and it has many indirect benefits that go along with it. For example, workers who give credit to fellow employees have been found to eventually make more money than those who try to take all the credit for a job. The old model of a hero at work was someone who could do everything him- or herself, even if it involved bulldozing people along the way. The new model of a hero at work is someone who is a good team player and who gives credit where credit is due. A humble person makes friends at work, and friends can lead to promotions and increased business.

As technology and change have accelerated, there has become an increasing need to get expert help from people in fields we don't know much about. The era where one person can know and do everything has passed. It's almost impossible to stay current in *one* area of expertise, much less several areas concurrently. With change as rapid as this, it takes humility to be able to ask for and receive the help one needs in order to stay competitive. Those people who are willing to receive help are soon able to achieve the results they desire, and those who think they know it all or are unwilling to ask for help are eventually left in the dust.

I first learned the value of humility in the first mastermind group I became part of. For those who don't know, a mastermind group consists of several people who get together to help each other achieve their goals. Since I graduated high school and college with a straight-A average, I had become a bit cocky when it came to thinking I always knew what was best. So, when four people approached me to be in a mastermind group, I figured I'd be a nice guy and help them all out a bit. As we each took turns identifying problems in our business and asking for help, I got a bit snooty. The other members of the group had such simple problems to solve, and I was amazed at how they could have overlooked them. I showered them with my words of wisdom, and they were very grateful.

Then it was my turn to ask for help. I didn't really think they could help me out because my business problems were more complex, and besides, I was already doing *everything* possible to make things better. Wrong! The members of my mastermind group probably felt the same thing about me that I had felt about them. I think they thought I must have been a bit "slow" not to know how to better handle the problems I presented. I was amazed by how much I learned from their counsel. As I implemented their advice, my business grew much more quickly. I had learned the value of being humble and receiving outside help.

Humility does not mean that you go around feeling like you're worthless. It simply means that you recognize your own limitations, ask for advice when needed, and give credit to others when they've helped you out. People who know they need assistance and are willing to ask for it are at a great advantage in today's business climate. An easy way to experience humility is to simply *ask* others for help with your business (or other) concerns and problems. I often ask people questions such as, "What do you think is the best thing to do in this situation?" Two heads are indeed better than one. As you allow yourself to be humble and receive help when necessary, you'll notice that there will be great dividends at work.

❧ ❧ ❧

To cultivate the five "soul traits" I've presented here, one must act like a gardener, consistently weeding out whatever interferes with a productive planting season. The weeds in the way of growing our soul at work are things like too much "busy"ness, and going for quick fixes rather than living by enduring principles. Good gardeners also know how to properly "fertilize" and water the young plants they are trying to grow. In the case of manifesting your soul at work, watering and fertilizing can be done by using the many specific suggestions offered in this chapter. However, perhaps the most important ingredient of nourishing your inner (or regular) garden is consistency. Plants soon die or wither away if they're not watered. The soul at work will also wither away if it's not consistently attended to. After all, there are a lot of weeds out there. Take care of your "garden" at work, and it will take care of you.

❦ ❦ ❦

REAL WEALTH REMINDERS

1. There are many "characteristics" of the soul that are extremely valuable in the work environment. By tapping into things such as passion, creativity, selfless service, equanimity, and humility, people can experience more internal and external success while pursuing their careers.

2. For each soul trait I discuss, I offer a question you can ask yourself to help you toward tapping into this ability in your work. These questions are:

   • Passion—"How can I make money doing what I love and feel passionate about?"

   • Selfless service—"How can I give my customers (or employers) even more value than they could possibly expect?"

   • *Creativity*—"What's a creative way of handling this problem, or how could I be even more open to creativity in my work?"

   • *Equanimity*—"What could potentially be good about this?"

   • *Humility*—(asking others) "What do you think is best to do in this situation?"

By focusing on and receiving intuitive answers to these questions, you can benefit from the call of your soul at work.

3.   Just as flowers need to be watered and cared for, we need to consistently nourish the five "soul traits" above—or the weeds of ordinary working life will kill them off.

CHAPTER SIX

MAKING SPIRIT YOUR BUSINESS PARTNER

"Whenever you want to produce something, do not depend upon the outside source; go deep and seek the Infinite Source."
— Paramahansa Yogananda

Money is a form of energy. At one time we lived in an era when energy could easily be shown to obey certain rational laws. Sir Isaac Newton, with just a few crude instruments, plotted out the basic laws of physics. Then Einstein appeared. With the idea of relativity and quantum mechanics, Einstein showed that nothing is as rational or as linear as it seems. As it is with physics, so it is with money. On the surface, it seems that money is an entirely linear phenomenon. By that, I mean it should obey certain rational economic laws that anyone can master. Yet, my experience of working with thousands of people indicates that there is a lot more going on than meets the eye.

Do you know people who make a lot of money but are always just barely getting by? Conversely, do you know people who hardly make any money—but always seem to have enough? Experience shows us that some people struggle for years to master their finances but never do. On the other hand, some people seem to do just about everything wrong in a strict financial sense, but riches seem to follow them wherever they go. Why is that?

I think the "relativity" of money is due to the fact that some people have an "inside edge" when it comes to attracting wealth, while others don't. This inside edge is available to all those who are willing to look at money manifestation in a new way. From studying people who attract riches no matter what they do, I've noticed four common practices they use for attracting wealth through "nonlinear" or "spiritual" methods. We'll look at each of these practices and explore ways in which you can immediately begin using them in your own life.

#1: Intuition

Intuition means different things to different people. For some, it means the ability to listen to their innermost desires, feelings, and innate wisdom. For others, intuition is considered something that originates from an outside "force," such as God or a Higher Power. A definition I've found useful is the following: *Intuition is a realm of expanded information that people can tune in to once they've quieted their mind and let go of their need for their ego to be in control.* By using this definition, anyone can learn to tap in to a storehouse of beneficial information—once they know the right technique.

What keeps a lot of people from profiting from intuitive insights is lack of faith. While most individuals have had intuitive flashes at some point in their life, these experiences are often few and far between. On the other hand, we've been trained to handle situations through linear, rational thinking ever since we were babies. With so much practice, we've developed faith in the "left-brain" method for creating success. Indeed, such an approach is valuable and effective. But a "whole-brain" system for success is likely to reap even greater rewards. By tapping in to intuitive guidance and using this information in collaboration with analytical thinking, a whole new level of success and enjoyment is possible.

My first experience with combining intuitive information with linear, rational planning occurred with the video I produced: *Intimacy and Sexual Ecstasy*. As I mentioned in the introduction to this book, I came up with the concept for the video while meditating. In fact, about 70 percent of the final script was "given" to me while I sat in meditation. I knew the information that came through with such clarity and energy was something to take seriously. Yet, my second reaction to this idea was to begin doubting it. So I did a little research, which showed that there was a huge, largely untapped market for an educational video such as this one. My next reaction was a feeling of being overwhelmed. After all, I was broke and living in a beat-up 1967 Dodge van. How was I going to put such a massive project together? Once again, faith in my intuition was helpful. I kept getting the message to move forward and somehow things would fall into place.

Faith, to me, is the ability to believe in things that are unseen. I said to myself, "If you're meant to put this video together, then you'll get the help you need." I knew that if I didn't try, I'd feel like a failure. If I did try—and failed—then at least I would have learned something from my efforts. So I wrote down all the things I would need to do to accomplish this project. My list included over 50 small tasks. I even asked my intuition for direction on what steps I needed to take, and in which order I should take them. With faith in my inner guidance and my ability to act, I was able to overcome my fears and doubts. Because the video ended up being a huge success, my faith in the power of intuition has grown. Nowadays, I only do projects that have gotten a "go-ahead" from the still, small voice within.

Hopefully, you're sold on the benefits of tapping in to your own inner guidance. But how can you tell the difference between true intuition and thoughts that stem from your ego mind? There's no one simple answer, but there are guidelines. First of all, you're more likely to be open to the still, small voice within if you deliberately set out to quiet your mind. I believe that each person is equipped with a built-in method for becoming peaceful. If you like to meditate, then meditate. If after jogging, dancing, or exercise you feel relaxed and quiet inside, then do that. Or if being in a certain place in nature refreshes and calms your soul, then proceed to your special spot. Ultimately, your intention to quiet your mind and listen to your intuition is just as important as the approach you use.

After working with thousands of people in seminars, I have found one thing in particular that helps people quickly and easily quiet their mind: music. More specifically, if you listen to a couple of your favorite songs that are meaningful to you, you'll find that they can immediately help you quiet your mind and open your heart.

Once you've completed an activity or used a technique to quiet your mind, then you're ready to ask "power questions." Power questions are inquiries whose answers could significantly impact your life. My book *Instant Insight: 200 Ways to Create the Life You Really Want* is filled with power questions that help guide people to important realizations. Each day when I meditate, I ask my intuition at least one of these questions. Below is a list of such questions having to do with money and career issues:

1. How can I use the gifts I've been given to make money and serve the Universe?
2. What can I do to be of greater value at work?
3. What do I need to know (or do) to experience more peace around my money/work issues?
4. In what creative ways could I increase my income?
5. Would focusing on [fill in the blank] be for my highest good at this time?
6. What do I need to know to take the next successful step

toward [fill in the blank]?

7. [Come up with your own question to suit your specific needs.]

When tapping in to my intuition, I try to let go of all my rational thoughts and comments concerning the question I've asked. There's a difference between hearing your inner guidance and figuring something out rationally. Some people report that they receive their intuitive flashes in the form of symbols or images. Other people say that they actually hear a "still, small voice." In my own case, I usually tap in to this form of spiritual information through an "Ah-hah" experience. I simply keep repeating the question to myself, and then suddenly I just *know* the answer. It's usually quite exhilarating. With practice, you'll begin to notice that you have a favorite way of receiving intuitive guidance. There is no single correct way. Whatever works for you is a valid method.

Frequently, my intuition has nothing to say when I first ask it a question. But if I keep on asking, an answer is almost always forthcoming—sometimes when I least expect it. A couple of years ago, I wanted to know if I should go to India to visit some spiritual teachers I know there. I asked my intuition but got nothing for several days. In order to get a discount fare, I had to decide by the end of the month. On the last day of the month as I was TV channel-surfing, I almost skipped past a preacher's show, but my intuition clearly told me to switch back and listen to the man (something I rarely do). The first thing this pastor said was, "You need to go to India." I thought this was an interesting coincidence, so my ears perked up. He then went on to say, "You need to spend a month in India to see how these people live." Then there was a close-up of the preacher's face, and I clearly heard him say, "Jonathan, you *especially* need to go to India." I practically fell off my chair. I bought my tickets immediately.

If your reaction to that story is disbelief, then you underestimate the power of intuition. Of course there is no rational explanation for how this preacher could, on national television, call out my name and give me a direct message. But we live in a magical Universe. Although I have no idea *how* such things happen, I've had enough of these experiences to know that they *do indeed* occur. I don't even know how my TV works, but I have faith that if I do certain things (such as turn it on), I can tune into worlds and pictures that seem to materialize out of thin air.

When you ask your intuition a question with enough sincerity and intensity, you open yourself up to a whole new way of receiving valuable information. If you don't get your answer immediately, look for any strange coincidences or "messages" in your life. The answer may come from a friend's words, a book, a passing billboard, or from deep within. If you don't have the answer within a week, you might ask, "Is the information I'm requesting good for me to know at this time?" I have seen that there are times when it has actually been best for me *not* to know the answer to the question I asked. By asking if your question is appropriate, you can check to see if there's a reason why you're not receiving an answer. There's an old adage that says, "The Lord works in mysterious ways." By listening to your intuition, you'll see that such a statement is true.

#2: Dreams and Rest

The idea for the sewing machine came to a young tailor in a dream. Many Nobel Prize–winning scientists have said that a critical aspect of their discoveries came to them while taking a nap. In the Bible, many of the prophets received their revelations during their dreamtime encounters. Dreams are a doorway to the subconscious mind, and if you've ever analyzed your dreams, you know that the subconscious can be very ingenious and creative. During the night, the subconscious is let loose. Without the usual restrictions and worries to burden it, the subconscious can creatively work on problems and ideas even though your body is fast asleep.

Times of daydreaming and rest can also be important ways for the subconscious to unleash its power. You've probably heard of people who have had the solution to a problem constantly evade them, only to have it magically appear while walking their dog. The subconscious never rests. With the "noise" of the rational mind temporarily quieted during times of relaxation, the subconscious is more likely to be heard. In addition, Spirit can sometimes get a message through to our subconscious mind that can later penetrate our conscious mind. Prophetic or divinely inspired dreams are an example of this type of experience in action. With practice and the right techniques, your sleep and relaxation time can become some of the most productive moments you have!

In order to solve problems and receive divine guidance during your dreamtime, a couple of methods are helpful. First, it will be useful to keep a dream journal. Dreams respond to your attention. If your subconscious knows that you're on the lookout for important information, your dreams will actually become more interesting and meaningful. Keep the journal and a pen right by your bed, and the moment you wake up, write down anything you can remember. If you're as groggy as I am when you first wake up, you might consider having a cassette player by your bed. By doing so, all you need to do is press the "record" button and say whatever you remember.

You can increase the likelihood of your dreams and rest time being productive by repeating a question you'd like an answer to just before falling asleep. For example, if you would like to know how you can make more money, simply repeat, "How can I make more money doing what I love?" as you drift off. Eventually, your subconscious and/or Spirit will respond. The same holds true during times of relaxation. Simply repeat a question you'd like an answer to, without any attempt to answer it rationally. Then, simply wait for Grace to shower down upon you. With practice, your subconscious will realize you're actually paying attention, and like a dog that is eager to please, it will do its best to make you happy.

#3: *Making Deals With "God"*

A third way to tap in to a nonlinear way of making money is to make a "deal" with "God" (or your Higher Self). The way to do this is simply to state the terms of the pact out loud or on paper. For example, one pledge I made with God proclaimed that I would quit my job in order to work exclusively on the *Intimacy* video *if* I somehow received enough money to live on for three months. I made such a deal because my intuition was telling me to quit my job, but my mind was too afraid to take such decisive action without any source of income to cover my bills. I figured that I needed about three months to finish the video and begin to market it. Therefore, one day I went to a favorite nature spot, quieted my mind, and proclaimed the following: "If You want me to quit my job to focus on the video, arrange to have all my bills and rent paid for at least three months."

Five days later, I received a letter from my aunt. The note inside simply said, "When your grandma died [two years previously], she said to distribute some money she left for you whenever I felt it was the right time." Inside the envelope was a check for $5,000. I got down on my knees and thanked God for helping me, and I promised I would fulfill my end of the deal. I quit my job, made the video, and best of all, I discovered a new principle for manifesting miracles.

If you're skeptical about this method, then it simply means you haven't yet had a similar type of experience. You need not take my word for it that it can work. Try it yourself. That's the only way you'll be convinced. Having gone through this process many times, I've noticed that there are guidelines that can help you tap in to this magical process:

1. Only make deals you're willing to keep. If "God" comes through with the terms of the pact, then you absolutely must fulfill your end of the bargain.

2. The best time to make a deal with Spirit is when you intuitively think you're being directed toward a difficult course of action. The "deal" is basically your way of asking for confirmation and help with the task at hand.

3. Perform some ritual or go to a special place when proclaiming the terms of the arrangement. This will help you (and God?) know that a special covenant has been created.

4. Make the terms of the deal highly possible for both you and God. In other words, don't say, "I'll enter a monastery if you levitate me off the ground." Don't ask for more than you sincerely need.

5. Be specific as to when you want to see Spirit's end of the bargain fulfilled. Don't make it too difficult. Patience is often necessary to fulfill God's plan.

6. If God seemingly doesn't do what you requested, it might not mean that you shouldn't move forward with *your* end of the agreement. My experience is that Spirit can work on many levels. At times I've noticed that God didn't do what I requested, yet I received some *other* form of guidance that helped me know I was on the right course. Keep listening to your intuitive guidance for updates.

7. Use this process only when faced with truly important decisions or challenges. It's possible to diminish the power of this method by using it on trivial matters.

8. Don't use this method simply to get something for yourself. It's best to use it in the context of deciding how to use your gifts for service to yourself and humanity.

It's important to decide precisely what you want from God when you make a deal. Rather than ask for some outwardly dramatic sign, I usually just ask for an inward indication of what I should do. For example, at one time I was trying to decide between taking a ten-day meditation course or traveling for ten days. I thought the meditation course would do me more good, but it was the last thing in the world I wanted to do at the time. So I made a pact with God: "If You want me to take the meditation course, then I'll need You to change my feelings about taking it. If I wake up tomorrow and feel a *desire* to take it, then I'll follow Your wishes." When I woke up the next morning, my feelings had totally shifted. The idea of traveling seemed completely repulsive, whereas the idea of meditating struck me as truly exciting. Although it was simply a change in my perception, it was as dramatic a sign as receiving $5,000 in the mail.

Although this process may sound extremely far out, if you read almost any holy book, you'll find references to this "technique." If and when you use this manifestation process successfully, you will never be the same. It's exciting to *think* that a Universal force could interact with us in such an intimate manner. Yet, actually *experiencing* it is even more amazing. Best of all, making deals with God can help show you that, even in the world of material manifestations, Grace and magic can happen.

#4: Reading the Universe

A final way to make Spirit your business partner is to learn to read the subtler signs that the Universe (God) sends your way. In the previous section, I discussed how you could ask for a specific sign from the Universe. This is particularly helpful when you need to make an important decision that you're a bit hesitant about. When "reading the Universe," you learn to watch for the little signs that are *always* coming your way. It's a lot like the hot and cold game I talked about in chapter 4. I believe that when we're on course, Spirit can let us know by having strange coincidences occur, or by making things happen smoothly and easily. Such things tell us we're "warmer" or more in alignment with God's will. On the other hand, when we're off course, Spirit can send us a "cooler" message by making things seem difficult or feel meaningless.

It takes courage and willingness to receive the message that you're freezing or off course. The world is always giving us clues to set us straight, but we're not always ready to receive them. The defenses of blame, denial, distraction, and belief do more than keep us from seeing our own shortcomings. They can also prevent us from recognizing signs that tell us we're getting closer or farther away from alignment with God's will. For example, I had a psychotherapy client who was always sick on Mondays. She *denied* that it had anything to do with the fact that she hated her job, and instead *blamed* her illness on weekly hormonal imbalances. Of course, once she summoned up the courage to change her job, her weekly hormonal imbalance somehow magically cleared up!

There is no foolproof way to accurately interpret the subtle signs that the Universe sends your way. Yet, there are helpful guidelines. First, it helps to be free of any strong bias that might make it harder to interpret or listen to the signs that exist. In order to listen to what Spirit is trying to tell us, we have to be open to *whatever* it might indicate. My client who hated her job didn't recognize her weekly illness as a sign because she was too afraid to look for another job. In addition, she believed that money would become a big problem if she tried to find a new line of work. Her belief and her fear created a bias too strong for her to receive any new information.

Several years ago, I got an order from a video catalog that wanted to buy several thousand of my videos. When I talked to the buyer of this company, I got a bad feeling about him. Yet, I denied the feeling and shipped the 3,000 videos that were ordered. When it came time for the company to pay their bill of $15,000, they declared bankruptcy. My desire for the money blinded me to my gut feelings about this company. Had I not had such a strong desire to sell the tapes, I would have listened to my feelings and avoided the entire transaction. It was an expensive lesson!

After my experience with the videos, I have made a point of listening to my intuition, feelings, and hunches—even if I don't like what I "hear." Nowadays, if I have a bad feeling about a certain person, I proceed very cautiously. I may spend additional time researching if he or she is the right person to do business with. Yet, I don't rely *only* on intuition and feelings. When making important decisions, I will usually begin by gathering all the relevant information I can. Then, when I finally *have* to make a decision, I bring the rational and intuitive parts of my brain together and see what feels right. I believe that two heads, or using *both* sides of our brain, is indeed better than one. Only when we use our intuitive right brain coupled with our analytical left brain can we create a full picture of what's before us. From this "big picture," we can make the best possible decisions.

If you're faced with a major decision and you've accumulated all the rational and intuitive information you can, but things still aren't clear, there are additional things you can do. First, check to see if you've really surrendered this decision to Spirit. It could be that your desires are interfering with getting clear about what you need to do. Second, talk to a trusted friend about what you're experiencing. Sometimes he or she will say exactly what you need to hear to gain the clarity you seek. Third, as I previously discussed, you can always make a deal with God. If you're not sure what to do, you can say, "I think You want me to do option number one. If You really want me to do option number two, then let me know by somehow making that clear to me by this Sunday."

Last, but not least, you can go on a vision quest. A vision quest is an inner adventure designed for a specific purpose. Historically, people went on vision quests to help them make important decisions in their lives or to celebrate important transitions. I've found that the vision quests I've experienced have never failed to provide me with the clarity I was seeking. A vision quest can be made to the desert, the mountains, or any spot that has particular meaning for you. Simply making the journey to a distant location tells Spirit (and you) that you mean business. Once there, you can do whatever ritual helps you connect to your intuitive wisdom. Within a short period of time, you will likely notice that the clarity you seek has magically occurred. As the Bible says, "Seek and ye shall find."

Bringing Spirit into our money and work decisions can be frightening. Opening to the Universal Intelligence requires letting go of our tendency to control everything through our rational minds. Yet, making Spirit a business partner need not be an all-or-nothing experience. I believe we can begin by asking Spirit for guidance even though we are *still* making use of our rational minds. However, if we want inner guidance to *keep* coming to us, we need to occasionally take the chance to act on what it says. We need not exercise our faith beginning with major financial and career decisions. We can start with small decisions and let our faith in our business partner, Mr. or Ms. Spirit, gradually increase as we notice the results we receive. Spirit is always looking for a few good people to hire as employees to serve humanity. You now have several ways to let it be known to the Creator that you're available for a job.

REAL WEALTH REMINDERS

1. It's possible to make money simply by listening for intuitive information or Spirit's guidance. Creative ideas and projects born from such guidance can often be used to create success in the material world.

2. There are several ways to listen for and discern Spirit's guidance. Four simple ways include hearing your intuition, listening to your daydreams and night dreams, making "deals" with God, and properly interpreting the signs that the Universe sends your way.

3. Using both sides of your brain is likely to lead to better results than just listening to one source of information. By using your analytic, rational mind in combination with your spiritual, intuitive sense, you can make the best possible work-related decisions.

CHAPTER SEVEN

INNER AND OUTER GOALS

*"There are two ways to be happy. We may either
diminish our wants or augment our means. If you are wise,
you will do both at the same time."*

— Benjamin Franklin

How do you feel about setting goals? If you're like most spiritually minded people, you're just about ready to turn to the next chapter. Many people have the idea that setting goals is antispiritual. In actuality, almost all spiritual growth requires some sort of discipline. Goals are simply a method of disciplining yourself to achieve what's most important to you. Since the word *goals* can have a negative connotation for people, when I speak to groups I often substitute the phrase *manifesting your dreams* for *setting goals*. In this chapter, you will learn an efficient and time-tested process for manifesting your inner and outer dreams. In the end, having money isn't nearly as important as mastering the *process* of creating what you want in your life. Setting and achieving goals is perhaps the most documented technique for manifesting what you want—efficiently and effectively.

In 1953, a study was initiated at Yale University in which all the graduating students were asked if they had written down their goals. Approximately 3 percent had written down at least one goal. For 20 years they studied how these 3 percent fared in life as compared with the 97 percent of Yale graduates who didn't write down any goals that year. In 1973, when they surveyed how these two groups did, they found that the people who'd written down goals were reportedly happier than the rest. They also displayed better health, a lower incidence of divorce, and greater career satisfaction. The researchers even learned that the 3 percent who had written goals were worth more financially than the other 97 percent *combined*. That means they were making over 30 times the income of their classmates! Knowing what you want to create in your life and writing it down as a goal is a time-tested and powerful way to manifest your dreams.

Balanced Goals

Since writing down your goals is so powerful, it's important to know precisely what you want to create so you are satisfied when you get it. If you don't specify your dreams clearly enough, you can end up creating a nightmare. Sometimes people who write down their goals *do* create a life that is out of harmony. Why? Because their goals are all outward goals—such as wanting more money. Yet, manifesting more money is of little benefit if it's created at the cost of your time, relationships, and peace of mind. Therefore, I think it's best to create what I call "balanced goals," which are *goals that have both an internal and an external element to them.* For example, if you want more money, it can be helpful to know *why* you want it. If you realize it's to have more peace of mind, then why not make a goal of also creating more peace of mind in your life *while* you make more money?

There are many advantages to creating balanced goals. First

of all, by knowing both the internal and external target you're aiming for, it's more likely you'll hit the bull's-eye. Some people who only go for the external target, such as making money, end up completely missing the internal target. They make millions, but they don't get what they really want—such as more peace of mind. Another advantage of balanced goals is the fact that they help people experience what they truly desire more quickly. After all, people really *do* want more peace, and having more money is just *one* method of creating it. By exploring more ways to create inner peace, a person is almost certain to have greater success. A third advantage of balanced goals is that they help people to grow spiritually and financially at the same time. We don't want to create goals that impede our spiritual aspirations. Nor can we afford to ignore the challenges of the material world. Creating balanced goals is a way to produce balance within ourselves so we can better create harmony in our lives.

Several years ago, I had a wealthy client named Steven who came to me for counseling. His stated goal was that he wanted to make more money. After asking him a few questions, I found out that he made over $200,000 a year! When I asked him why he wanted more money, he said, "If I just had more money, I could finally get the respect and feeling of success I've always wanted."

From my perspective, he didn't need more money—he needed a greater sense of self-esteem. Yet, had I told him he needed to work on that internal goal, he probably would have walked out of my office. Instead, I suggested that we create a balanced goal. We authored a plan to raise his income and devised a separate plan for raising his self-esteem. The synergy of our two plans working together produced amazingly quick results. As he worked on his self-esteem, it resulted in his making more money, and as he made more money, it further elevated his self-esteem. Two goals working in sync are much better than one.

Outer Goals

Part of our journey as spiritual beings is to learn to manifest our deepest wants and needs on the material plane. An "outer goal" is simply a desire to realize something on the material plane—such as a new job or a house. As I mentioned in the introduction, my first major goal was to produce a video explaining how to create a successful intimate relationship. Because I had no money or collateral and I needed to raise $45,000, my task was not going to be easy. I began by writing down my goal, along with every possible action that might help me achieve it. I asked people who were experts in the art of raising money for their advice. From people with considerable business experience, I learned the importance of creating a business plan. I purchased a book on the subject in order to create such a strategy, and soon produced one. In my business plan, I outlined a system whereby investors would receive a percentage of profits from the video in exchange for their cash up front. In three weeks, by handing out my business plan to everyone I could think of, I had over $23,000 promised. Unfortunately, I then hit a wall.

Part of learning to manifest your dreams is being able to overcome the obstacles you inevitably face along the way. When I couldn't find any more investors, I initially felt defeated. I had previously vowed not to borrow any money from my family members, but now my resolve was wearing thin. No matter how many people I tried to enroll in the project, I couldn't get anyone else interested. Finally, I prayed for Divine guidance. To my surprise, the message I received was that I should begin the video with the money I had already collected. Somehow, I summoned the courage to follow the guidance I received, and I began the project. Three days later, seemingly out of nowhere, several investors called me and offered me $60,000 more. I actually had to turn down investors because I had too much money! Intuitively, I felt that my willingness to begin the project was the "magic spark" that created a firestorm of new investors calling me. The leap of faith I took back then of fully committing to the video even though I didn't have all the money is still affecting my life today. It's been eight years since the video was completed, and it's still bringing in a sizable amount of money for my investors and me.

෫ ෫ ෫

In my workshops, I have guided thousands of people through the process of "dream manifestation." I have seen what works and what does not. What follows is a brief description of five steps you can take to manifest whatever you desire. In this example, I will use the goals of a woman named Sarah, whom I recently worked with in my office:

Step #1: Write down a single goal you'd like to achieve. If you don't know what you'd like to manifest, answer the question, "If I could create or have anything, what would it be?" When I asked Sarah this question, she initially said she would like to have more money.

Step #2: Write down your criteria that the goal has been adequately achieved. A criterion of success would be a specific and measurable description of exactly what you want, and precisely when you want it. Of course, it's important that your goal be realistic and attainable based on the effort you're willing to put forth. Sarah decided that she'd like to increase her income by 30 percent within one year.

Step #3: Brainstorm steps you could take that would help you move toward achieving what you want. Ask other people how they might go about achieving a similar goal. The more ideas you come up with, the better. You should be able to fill in this sentence: "Six or more things I could do to help me on the path of achieving my goal include…" In the case of making 30 percent more money, Sarah's list of brainstorming ideas looked like this:

1. Work toward getting a promotion at work by finding out my boss's specific needs and by doing everything I can to impress him.

2. Make helpful suggestions to my boss's boss.

3. Work extra hours so that the quality of my work goes up.

4. Read a book on marketing so I can come up with ideas for selling more of our product.

5. Read a book on tapping into creativity so I can think of new ways to help the company.

6. Start writing articles that I can sell to a trade journal so I can make more money and become an expert in my field.

Step #4: From Step #3, create a logical order for doing the items you came up with on your brainstorm list. To do this, simply ask yourself, "Which item(s) would be best to do first, second, third, etc.?

Step #5: Evaluate what's working and what isn't, and make appropriate adjustments. Keep breaking the big goal down into small steps. Do each task in the order you think will work best for achieving the goal you desire.

That's all you need to do to manifest your dreams in the material world. It sounds easy, but there are many obstacles that can arise to make this process difficult. Some obstacles are unexpected events that life throws your way. For example, it would be harder to increase your income by 30 percent if your company downsized and laid you off. Yet, I've found that most of the obstacles that interfere with goal attainment are between our ears. What follows is a list of the 12 most common errors people make when trying to attain their goals:

Error #1: Forgetting to write down your goals, and/or not having clear criteria for their success—including when you would like your goal (or part of the goal) to be completed.

Error #2: Setting goals that are unrealistic in order to make up for all the time you may have wasted in the past. Unrealistic goals lead to discouragement when they are not met, and this could result in giving up completely.

Error #3: Setting too many goals at once in order to make up for being behind, which could lead to discouragement or a lack of focus.

Error #4: Failing to break each goal into small, easily doable steps. When you forget to do this, there is a tendency to become overwhelmed by the size of the task—and eventually to give up.

Error #5: Not having your step-by-step plan written down and in daily sight.

Error #6: Not being committed enough to overcome unanticipated obstacles.

Error #7: Forgetting to put the next step toward the completion of your goal on your calendar or "to do" list.

Error #8: Becoming too impatient to do just a little bit each week toward the completion of your goal, thereby becoming inconsistent in your actions.

Error #9: Failing to create an effective system to stay motivated and consistent in your actions until your goal is achieved.

Error #10: Lack of flexibility when something doesn't work quite right, which can lead to giving up instead of making the appropriate adjustments to your plan.

Error #11: Not asking other people or experts for help on how to best achieve your goal. Using an inefficient or unusable method in going about this task.

Error #12: Subconsciously believing a particular goal is not possible for you to achieve, thereby sabotaging your efforts.

If you're having difficulty achieving a goal, go through this list of common mistakes and see if you're making any of them. The fewer errors you make, the more likely it is that you'll achieve your goals efficiently and effectively.

Inner Goals

Because our culture is so externally focused, the concept of creating "inner goals" is not widely familiar. An inner goal is simply a desire to have more of a specific internal experience, or wanting to manifest more of a particular trait. For example, you might want to be more loving, more kind, experience more peace, feel less anger, or enjoy a deeper sense of freedom. An easy way to get in touch with an important internal goal is to ask yourself, "If I could choose one thing about myself I'd like to change, or one thing I'd like to experience more of, what would it be?" Whatever your answer is to that question, you could make that an inner goal.

Previously I mentioned the value of creating balanced goals—an external and internal goal that both point to the same target. To create a balanced goal, you need to know two things. First, you need to know exactly what you'd like to manifest in the material world. Second, you want to identify what you hope to experience as a result of achieving your external goal. In the last section, we used the example of someone I worked with named Sarah who wanted to increase her income by 30 percent. When Sarah was in my office, I asked her, "*Why* do you want to increase your income by 30 percent?" She replied, "So I can finally buy my own house." Then I asked her, "Why do you want to buy your own house?" She thought about it for a moment and said, "So I can create a truly comfortable environment and feel more secure."

Sarah really desired a greater feeling of comfort and security in her life. Making a higher income was only the means to an end. Since she knew what she ultimately wanted, I suggested that she make *that* her inner goal. Sarah's initial response to my suggestion was, "How can you do that?" I replied, "If you knew you were going to be given a million dollars if you honestly felt more comfort and security in your life two months from now, could you figure out a way to feel more of those feelings?" Sarah immediately responded, "Sure." The truth is, if there is a big enough *reason* to achieve an inner goal, we can always find a way to create it in our lives. By having Sarah set both an external and internal goal pointed toward the same experience, she was able to experience what she wanted more quickly and easily.

Another advantage of creating balanced goals is the fact that they help people stay on course while they pursue material prosperity. Many people who try to make more money or be successful end up forgetting what it's all for. They lose track of the fact that they're really after a specific internal experience. It's a sad truth that a lot of people pursue money so they can have more peace and freedom, only to end up with millions of dollars...and millions of worries and burdens. By first getting clear on the ultimate experience you want to have and pursuing that experience as an ongoing goal, you are much more likely to create both wealth and peace.

The easiest way to know what inner goal is appropriate for you is to ask yourself the following question: "What feeling do I hope to experience as a result of achieving my external goal (such as more money, a house, etc.)?" Once you know the answer to that question, make having more of that experience the focus of your inner goal. Below is an example of how you might go through the five-step process for achieving an inner goal. To better illustrate this process, I'll use my interaction with Sarah as an example.

Step #1: Write down your inner goal. Ask yourself: "What feeling do I hope to experience as a result of achieving my external goal?" When I asked Sarah this question, she eventually realized that she wanted more comfort and security.

Step #2: Write down the criterion that determines whether the goal has been adequately achieved. In the case of inner goals, I suggest that people create an "intuitive scale" to measure how they're doing. Ask yourself, "On a 1 to 10 scale (10 representing the best that's possible), how much of my inner goal (in Sarah's case, how much comfort and security) do I currently have in my life?" When I asked Sarah this question, she said she was "about a 4." Then I asked her, "Where do you want to be on a 1 to 10 scale, and by when?" She responded, "I'd like to be at a level 7 five months from today."

Step #3: Brainstorm steps you could take to help you move toward your goal. Ask other people how they might go about achieving a similar goal. The more ideas you come up with, the better. You should be able to fill in this sentence: "Six or more things I could do to help me on the path of achieving my goal are…" When I asked Sarah this question, she came up with the following list:

1. Ask people who experience a deep sense of comfort and security in their lives what their secret is.

2. Learn to meditate so I can quiet my mind and feel more secure within myself.

3. Listen to hypnosis tapes to quiet my mind and feel less worry.

4. Take a self-defense class so I know I can always defend myself if I have to.

5. Read a book on confidence so I can feel more comfortable in social situations.

6. Ask two friends what they think would help me increase the level of comfort and security I feel in my life.

Notice that in the above example, I had Sarah create an internal way to measure her progress toward more security and comfort. You can always improve what you can measure. Although creating an "intuitive 1 to 10 scale" is not absolutely precise, people say that it works surprisingly well in measuring their progress. All you need to do is rate, on an internal 1 to 10 scale, how you're currently doing in the area you want to work on. Then, about once a week ask yourself, "How am I now doing (on a 1 to 10 scale)?" Hopefully, you'll see gradual improvement. If not, it may mean you need to do different tasks in order to be more successful.

For best results, keep your goals on a sheet of paper that you can see every day. About once a week or so, read over your plan and determine how you're doing. See if you can schedule any more steps from your plan into the upcoming week.

By taking small actions each week on her internal and external goals, Sarah was able to achieve both of them. In fact, she achieved her internal goal (creating more comfort and security) much faster than she expected. Sarah reported to me that her newfound comfort level assisted her on her job, which eventually led to the increase in pay. When people create balanced goals, they often work in a synergistic manner that leads to extraordinary results.

Imagined Experience

An additional aid to accomplishing your goals is to periodically imagine them as completed. Researchers have shown that your body can't tell the difference between *imagining* performing an action and actually doing it. In a classic study, one group of people was allowed to throw basketball free throws for 30 minutes a day. Another group simply *imagined* throwing free throws, while a third group did nothing. At the end of one week, the group that had thrown free throws and the group that had simply *visualized* throwing them both had improved the *same amount*. The group that had done nothing, the "control" group, predictably showed no improvement.

What do you think would happen if you took five minutes each day and clearly imagined yourself getting sick? Most people would be unwilling to do this because they intuitively know it would probably work. Yet, we forget to do the opposite—imagining what we want most in life. Studies such as the one with the basketball free throws show that what the mind can imagine and believe, it can achieve. Imagining your goal(s) already achieved is very similar to prayer. It gives the subconscious mind (and perhaps, God) a message as to exactly where you want to go.

Over the last two decades, a lot has been written about the power of visualization and prayer. But, as with any new technology, in recent years several new methods and ideas have been born that make the art of imagined experience more powerful than ever. In the 1970s, a method known as Neuro Linguistic Programming (NLP, for short) was born. Part of the theoretical foundation of NLP was that people create or imagine inner experiences in different ways. For example, take a moment now to remember, as fully as you can, what it was like to graduate from high school. Close your eyes now and think back.

How did you recreate that experience? Did you primarily visualize it? Or did you remember the sounds and speeches of that day? Perhaps you simply tuned into what it *felt* like. Each person has a unique way of imagining events. The creators of NLP noticed that people could make remembering past events or creating future experiences more *real* simply by having them "turn up the intensity" of their pictures, sounds, and feelings.

Imagine that you have a TV remote or dial that makes your inner pictures brighter and bigger. Envision a similar knob for turning up the sound, and a third dial for increasing the intensity of your feelings. Now, go back to imagining your high school graduation and see if by turning up your various "knobs," you can make the memory of that event more "real" for you. With a little practice, you'll probably find some particular adjustment with the dials that makes your memories really come to life. First, try making the pictures bigger and brighter. Next, see if you can play back the sounds in stereo. Keep playing with your imagination until the experience seems even more powerful. When you know how to turn up the intensity on your inner experiences, you can use this ability to help make your hopes and dreams become a reality. The clearer you can picture and feel your dreams, the easier it will be to achieve them.

The most important aspect of this form of prayer and visualization is to be able to feel—at the deepest level—that you can do whatever you visualize. In my workshops, I encourage participants to tune into the "specific vibration" of what living their dream would feel like. With practice, you can tune your mind and body in to specific frequencies—just like a radio. As you tune in to a beneficial frequency, such as the vibration of being fully abundant, you will find that money easily flows in your direction.

Leaders in just about every field will tell you that they "knew" they'd someday succeed. After all, they had already pictured and lived their success clearly and powerfully within their own minds. Whatever the mind fully believes, the body can achieve. Try it for yourself, and turn your dreams into reality!

REAL WEALTH REMINDERS

1. By creating both internal and external goals that point to what you desire, you can manifest your dreams effectively and efficiently.

2. To achieve your desired goals, list on paper what you'd like to create, your criteria for success, and the precise steps you can take to manifest your dream. Then, do the small steps in a logical order, and periodically evaluate your progress. Make sure you avoid the 12 errors people commonly make when trying to achieve their goals.

3. When creating an inner goal, ask yourself, "If I could choose one thing about myself I'd like to change, or one thing I'd like to experience more of, what would it be?" Use an intuitive (1 to 10) scale to measure your progress, and advanced visualization methods to help motivate you to stay on course.

CHAPTER EIGHT

THE POWER
OF YOUR WORD

"A lot of people know what to do,
but few people do what they know."

— Anthony Robbins

Imagine you're on a rocket ship, and you're trying to reach the moon. Making it to the moon represents the manifestation of all your material desires. In chapter 6, I presented nonlinear or spiritual methods to make your rocket ship soar faster and farther. In chapter 7, I discussed how to keep your rocket ship on course as it makes its journey. This chapter is about learning how to give your rocket all the fuel it will need to reach the moon. No matter how sophisticated a rocket is, it's worthless if it doesn't have enough fuel to go the distance.

What one trait would you say practically guarantees success in any field? Talent? Leadership? Knowledge? In my opinion, the single most important trait for guaranteed success is the ability to be *consistent* in one's efforts. From Thomas Edison to Mother Teresa, the most successful people in any field are those who can stay motivated over a long period of time. That's why people who love their jobs tend to do better financially than those who don't.

They are simply more consistent in their efforts. Unfortunately, people have a hard time maintaining high levels of motivation and effort over a long period of time. For most people, the inability to consistently act on their plans is what ultimately defeats them. Yet, there is now a method that is so simple and effective for overcoming this problem that, if you use it, your life will never be the same.

Before divulging the technique for maintaining high levels of motivation and effort, let me briefly tell you how I created it. I noticed in my work as a psychotherapist that people usually know exactly what they need to do to improve their lives or financial conditions. The problem is *they just don't do it.* A basic rule of psychology is that people act to avoid *immediate* pain and/or gain *immediate* pleasure. For example, people who have a history of going into debt using credit cards know that using them is bad for their financial health. But they still use them. Why? Because charging items helps them avoid immediate pain (that is, feeling they can't afford something) and leads to immediate pleasure (a new purchase). However, the *long-term* pain of irresponsible credit card use is to be forever trapped in debt, but since that pain is not as immediate, people continue to abuse credit cards.

I realized that, for people to make consistent progress toward their goals, they would need some form of immediate pain (or punishment) to occur if they failed to take appropriate action. For example, you probably know you *ought to* exercise more regularly and/or eat more healthfully, but because there is no immediate punishment for failing to exercise, you're not as consistent as you'd like to be. Now if every time you failed to exercise three times a week some guy came over and punched you, you'd be a lot more consistent. For better or worse, you're probably reluctant to hire a person to physically harm you if you don't follow through on your goals. Therefore, you need to find an immediate punishment you'd be willing to *give to yourself* if you fail to act in beneficial ways.

After much trial and error, I found a solution that worked. I call it the I.C.A.N. method, which is an acronym for Integrity Contract and Nurturance method. In the last three years, I've taught this process to thousands of people, and the results have been astounding. Of all the psychological methods I've ever come across, I've never seen any technique have as much impact as this one. In order for this method to create amazing changes in your life, you don't have to have faith in it, you don't have to believe in it, and you don't even have to like it. You just need to use it. Here's the essence of the technique:

Write a contract with yourself that states all the precise actions you're willing to commit to do during the following week. Then write a statement that says, "For each of the items on this contract that I fail to complete by one week from today, I agree to rip up two dollars." Finally, sign your contract, date it, and place it in a place you'll see it every day. That's it. Here's an example of a simple contract: "During the next week, I will exercise three times for a minimum of 40 minutes. I will read a minimum of 60 pages from the book I bought on investing. I will call at least five people about buying the widgets I just got in. For each task I don't complete by September 27, I will rip up two dollars."

Tearing up money is not a fun thing to do. I have hundreds of stories of people who have altered the course of their lives to avoid ripping up two dollar bills. I've used this technique to get people off heroin and cigarettes. I've used this method to get people to exercise consistently so they could lose weight. I've used this method to help people increase their income 500 percent in one year. It works with lazy people, it works with motivated people, it even works for people who are absolutely sure that it won't work for them. Basically, if you use it, it will work.

Some people worry that it might be illegal to rip up money. To determine if this was true, I called the Secret Service. After talking to four employees who didn't know if it was legal or not, I talked to one of the top guys there. He said, "I guess it's okay as long as it's your money. I've been here for over 30 years, and no one has ever even asked such a question!"

There are several reasons why this method is so effective. First, there is a clear proclamation of what you intend to do, and by what date you intend to do it. Normally, people have a lot of lofty *thoughts* about what they could do to improve their lives, but these thoughts soon slip away. With the I.C.A.N. method, you'll have a visual reminder of what you're *committed* to do. Second, with this technique, you'll experience immediate punishment if you fail to keep your word. Since your brain is always trying to avoid pain and suffering, it will do its best to complete what's on the contract.

You might be wondering, why rip up two dollars? Why not one dollar or five dollars? Having used this method with countless people over the years, I've seen that two dollars usually works best. When people write down that they'll rip up a five-dollar bill for each incomplete task, when push comes to shove, they often fail to rip up the money. Instead, they make excuses as to why they couldn't finish their contract, or they just blow the whole thing off rather than rip up that bill. Basically, their integrity is not worth a full five dollars. On the other hand, some people find that the threat of ripping up a single dollar isn't enough money to keep them motivated. However, most people find the pain of ripping up two dollars enough to get the job done, but if they don't complete their contract, they're willing to rip up the money to avoid going back on their word.

As far as I'm concerned, it's fine to not complete everything on your contract—as long as you rip up the money for the tasks you don't finish. I've seen that as long as people are willing to rip up money for failing to complete their contract, the method eventually works. Maybe not the first or second week, but by the third week you'll find your mind screaming at you to complete whatever you wrote down. After a while, the I.C.A.N. method becomes a trusted friend. You rely on it to help you do all the important things you used to procrastinate about. As an added bonus, this technique helps you build confidence. You begin to see that you can manifest whatever you desire simply by stating what you're committed to doing each week, and keeping your word.

What follows is a step-by-step account of how you can use the I.C.A.N. method each week to create what you desire in life:

1. Do something to quiet your mind. When you have done so, ask yourself, "What important things could I do this week to create a life of even more inner and outer riches?" Write down whatever ideas you come up with.

2. For the two, three, or four best ideas you think of from question #1, create simple, measurable tasks you can do within the course of a single week. For example, the inner message to "treat my customers better" might lead to giving them a sincere compliment when you interact with them. To increase your business exposure, you could put on your contract the task of giving out your business card to four potential customers.

3. Write down on a single sheet of paper all the specific things you plan to do by the end of one week. Then, state that for each item you fail to complete by the end of the week, you will rip up two dollars. Sign and date your contract. Below is an example of how such a contract looks.

I, Jonathan, agree to do the following over the course of the next week:

a. Call five potential clients about my new seminar.
b. Wash my car and put an ad in the paper to sell it.

c. Ask a friend to read my latest article and get his or her feedback.

d. Start a savings account to accumulate money for a vacation to Europe.

e. Meditate at least 30 minutes each day.

For each of the above items I fail to complete by 5:00 P.M. next Thursday, I agree to rip up two dollars.

_____   _____

Date   Signature

4. Put the contract in a place where you'll see it on a daily basis. Bathroom mirrors are good. So are car dashboards. If you have an appointment book, make sure you write down the exact time you plan to evaluate your contract. It's important that you schedule this. If possible, make this appointment exactly one week from the date of the writing of the contract.

5. At the end of the week, evaluate how you did. If you didn't complete any items on your contract, no matter what your excuse, tear up the appropriate amount of money. It may take a while to write contracts that work just right for you. Go through this process again for the upcoming week. Write a new contract that takes into account what worked for you in the previous week and what did not. After a few weeks, you'll find that you can write highly beneficial contracts in a matter of two or three minutes. If you find that you always miss items on your contract, then write easier contracts. On the other hand, if you find that you always complete everything, put a couple of more difficult items on your list. Have fun.

Ⓒ Ⓒ Ⓒ

I'll share with you a couple of ways in which this method has made me more money and has improved the quality of my life. In 1992, when I got the idea to interview spiritual leaders for my *Bridges to Heaven* book, I was initially overwhelmed by the task. I knew that contacting dozens of prominent people would be difficult, and I already had a full-time psychotherapy practice. Yet, I also knew that with the I.C.A.N. method, anything is possible. Without the contract, I would have simply kept myself busy with less important matters. Yet *with* the contract, I was able to consistently make progress on the book by working on it for two hours each week. Two years after beginning the project, the book was published.

In the last chapter, you came up with ideas and goals that are important to you. Think of how quickly you could turn them into a reality if you made progress on them each and every week. After a while, the I.C.A.N. method becomes a fun game you play with yourself. Rather than always putting off the dreams you have, it allows you to act on them right now. People who have the patience to slowly but surely make progress on their goals are the people who succeed in life.

In chapter 7, I talked about how my client, Sarah, set the goal to increase her income by 30 percent, and set another goal to feel more comfort and security in her life. Although setting goals is important, it was Sarah's consistent actions that allowed her to succeed. From her brainstorm list of small steps she could take, she would often put one or two items on her weekly contract. By making consistent progress, week after week, she was able to achieve her inner goal in a single month—rather than the five months she had anticipated. For her goal to increase her income by 30 percent, her consistent actions led to fruition within six months. Besides the fact that she was able to manifest her dreams so quickly, Sarah experienced a wonderful sense of confidence and accomplishment.

In seminars I lead about the I.C.A.N. technique, I am usually asked very similar questions. Therefore, what follows are the most common questions and their respective answers with respect to this process:

1. Why is it called the Integrity Contract and Nurturance method?

For two reasons. First, I wanted an acronym that would be easy to remember and would remind people what this method is for. The words *I can* aptly summarize the idea that whatever your goals are, they can be achieved through this process. Second, I included the words *integrity* and *nurturance* in the method's name to remind people *how* to properly use this process. This technique is really based on increasing your personal integrity, also known as the power of your word. I like to think that the ripping up of money isn't really a punishment, but rather an "integrity booster shot." By adhering to your contract, you increase your level of integrity, and thereby achieve greater personal power.

The word *nurturance* is used to signify that this method aims to nurture your dreams—not to make you feel guilty. Occasionally, people use the I.C.A.N. process to overwhelm themselves and make their lives unnecessarily difficult. If that's your experience with this process, then you're using it incorrectly. The goal of this method is to nurture the deepest desires you have for yourself and your life. By completing small tasks each week in the direction of your goals, you can make steady progress without feeling overwhelmed.

2. I find that I'm already too busy in my life. How can I add additional stuff without feeling even more burdened?

The contracting process requires you to decide what's *most important* to do each week. Typically, people get caught up in doing a lot of easy, but rather trivial stuff—and never spend time working toward what's *really* meaningful. The I.C.A.N. method can give you the power to get to the important stuff. Sometimes, this will mean that you leave some relatively unimportant things undone. Part of what makes this process so powerful is its requirement that you consciously *prioritize* the tasks in your life. It puts you firmly in control. If you feel as if you're doing too much, then you are even *more* in need of prioritizing the tasks in your life. No matter how busy you are, you always have time for what's *really* important. The I.C.A.N. process will simply have *you* decide what's important, rather than having the habits you've developed in the past determine your future.

3. **What do I do if an emergency comes up and I'm not able to complete the tasks on my contract?**

This is a tough question. I *used* to tell people that if any emergency comes up, just forget about your contract for that week. Then I noticed an interesting phenomenon. People were having emergencies on a weekly basis! When I'd ask what their emergency was, occasionally I'd hear excuses such as, "My mom called and upset me," or "I stubbed my toe." I even noticed that *I* was beginning to make slimy rationalizations to invalidate my contracts. Therefore, I now suggest that people specify the terms by which a contract can be made invalid. In my own case, at the bottom of my weekly contract I state: "This contract is invalid only under the following conditions":

- I am too sick to work for more than one day.
- I have to attend a loved one's funeral.
- I have an injury or illness that requires hospitalization.

As you can see, I give myself little leeway to excuse myself from my contracts. I suggest that you come up with specific conditions for which your contracts would be made invalid. Write them down. Don't underestimate how slippery your mind will be to try to avoid ripping up money. If your "emergency" isn't specified beforehand, then ripping up money is in order.

4. Instead of ripping up money, can I simply give it to a needy person or to a charitable organization?

In a word, NO. Part of the power behind this method is that it's quite painful to rip up money. You'll do a lot to avoid committing such a wasteful act. Last year, as an experiment, I allowed one group I worked with to give their money away instead of ripping it up. The results were disastrous. The effect of the I.C.A.N. process was diluted about 80 percent. Trust me on this one: Rip up the money if you don't complete the items on your contract.

If you simply can't get yourself to rip up two dollars for each broken agreement, then consider allowing yourself to rip up one dollar for missed contractual items. Some people have even successfully made contracts that state they'll throw away a mere 25 cents if they fail to complete an item on their contract. I suggest you start out with ripping up two dollars for each missed agreement, but after a couple of weeks, feel free to raise or lower that amount if you feel it would better suit your needs. If you find that you're starting to make excuses for why you're not completing your agreements, you're either making your contract too difficult or the amount you're ripping up is too high for you. Conversely, if you easily rip up money, you might try raising the price tag on each broken agreement to five dollars.

5. What items are best to put on a contract, and what is better left off?

If you ordinarily make five sales calls a week, there's no need to put that down on a contract. After all, you're already doing it. But if there's something you're not doing but you know it would benefit your financial life and/or well-being, then a contract will be of great benefit to you. Also, contracts are useful for breaking large goals into small tasks, which are easily accomplished within a week.

If you have a goal that is immense, then it doesn't belong on a contract. An example of this would be selling your house. Putting such a large goal on a weekly contract would simply add unnecessary pressure. Instead, ask yourself, "How could I break this into several smaller steps?" Tasks such as "Talk to three Realtors" and "Call for an appraisal" might be appropriate tasks that will move you in the right direction.

6. Why are contracts always for one week? Why not for one day or one month?

Experience has shown me that a single week works best. We tend to think in week-long increments, divided up between five days of work and a two-day weekend. When people have to make contracts for a longer period of time, the result has been less focus and more broken agreements. If you try to make contracts for less than a week's time, you'll spend all your time writing contracts—instead of taking action.

7. How many items are best to put on the contract?

I suggest that people begin with no more than two or three tasks on each weekly contract. Then, once you get used to that, feel free to slowly add additional items. Currently, I put about 20 tasks on my weekly contract, but I've been doing this for over five years. It's important that you don't use this process to overwhelm yourself. First build a momentum of successes. Once you're involved in a successful routine, you're ready to gradually add additional (and/or more difficult) tasks.

8. I sometimes forget to evaluate my contract at the end of the week. What can I do to make sure I remember to do this?

First, it's important to realize that your problem can simply be a creative way of resisting this very powerful process. Since this technique can dramatically alter your life, it's not unusual that some form of resistance will appear—at least initially. But once you've done this method for a month or so, your subconscious mind will notice that it really improves your life, and therefore will resist it less.

Many people have found that coming up with a specific time for writing and evaluating contracts helps them be consistent. For example, if you always complete this process on a Sunday night, or before work on Monday morning, you'll be less likely to forget. Second, you can add to your contract the caveat that if you fail to evaluate your progress on the specified date, you have to rip up an additional two dollars. Finally, it can really help to do the I.C.A.N. process with a friend.

From my experience of overseeing the I.C.A.N. process with thousands of people, I can say that the single most important way to ensure its success is to do it with a partner. When people try this process on their own, they frequently fail to rip up the appropriate amount of money. Yet, when you're accountable to someone else, it's a different story. Partners keep each other honest. You can also ask your partner to give you valuable feedback about how you use the process, or to act as a "judge" when you aren't sure if you completed the terms of your agreement. I have always done the I.C.A.N. process with a partner. I've noticed that it not only motivates me, but also leads to a deeper friendship.

When I get together with my partner to go over the contract, it doesn't take long. Sometimes we meet over breakfast, and sometimes we just check in over the phone. He asks me, "How'd you do this week?" In a typical week I might say, "I missed one item, and I already ripped up the money." Then I ask him, "How about you?" After he answers me, we sometimes ask each other what our focus is for the following week. Whenever possible, we hand or fax each other a copy of the next week's contract, and part ways. When we complete this process by phone, it literally takes two minutes. In the last three years, we've both raised our incomes rather dramatically as we've practiced increasing the power of our integrity and our word.

In order to find an appropriate partner, think of people who have goals they'd like to achieve. Then, simply let them read this chapter to see if they'd like to undertake this endeavor with you. Once you find one person who likes the idea and is willing to give it a try, you're set to begin. I've seen successful partnerships occur between parents and their children, married couples, friends, and even complete strangers randomly assigned to each other in my workshops. If you can manage to make it through the first month, you'll likely become hooked because you'll be so pleased by the results you're getting.

Soul Power

Throughout the history of our country, success in business was largely determined by an individual's reputation. Furthermore, the reputation of a business or a person was dependent on reliability, honesty, and trust. In the last 40 or so years, it may seem as if keeping one's word is not the powerhouse it used to be. That is a mistaken notion. Although individuals and businesses can survive without a superlative reputation for keeping their promises, they can never thrive. A reputation for dependability can be cashed in at the bank.

Although reliability and keeping one's word is valued in business, most people have never known of a systematic way of "exercising" this soul trait. Without regular exercise, our bodies become flabby. In the same way, unless we somehow exercise the power of our word (by making and keeping promises), we tend to become weak in this area. I consider the I.C.A.N. process to be as much a spiritual growth technique as a way of getting one's goals accomplished. I've seen that the method has a profound internal effect on most of the people who practice it. They become more honest, capable, and trustworthy. They create power in the world of Spirit as well as in the world of matter.

REAL WEALTH REMINDERS

1. The single most important trait for guaranteed success, whether materially or internally, is the ability to be consistent in one's efforts. Normally, this doesn't happen, because people would rather do things to experience short-term pleasure than feel that they are being punished in some way. Being consistent can be quite difficult (painful) for people.

2. By making a contract that lists several tasks you're willing to do over the course of a week, and stating that you'll rip up two dollars for each item you don't complete, you'll become more motivated to work on the most important goals in your life.

3. The I.C.A.N. method helps to strengthen the power of your word and boost your integrity. By creating weekly contracts with a partner, you'll have a systematic way to develop the personal power necessary for spiritual growth and continual success.

CHAPTER NINE

MARKETING YOUR DREAM

"Far and away the best prize that life offers is the chance to work hard at work worth doing."

— Theodore Roosevelt

In 1988, while meditating in my van, I received an idea for bringing billions of people together to pray for world peace and goodwill to all. The plan was simple: During the opening and closing ceremonies of the Olympic games, three billion people (over half the people on Earth) are simultaneously watching TV. My idea was to have an announcer tell the viewing audience to focus on their desire for peace and goodwill during a minute of silence. Once this brief meditation was over, the people in the stadium and the viewers at home would all sing a familiar song together. Finally, kids from every country in the world would join hands on the stadium field and sing another inspiring song.

When I received this vision while meditating, it rattled me to the core. I knew that having three billion people simultaneously linked in mind and heart would be an extremely powerful experience. Then, I came out of meditation and reality hit me. I was just a young man living in a van. How could *I* be the motivating force behind such an enormous event?

I believe that when we're given a dream or passion that inspires us, Spirit can help us out if we're willing to do some legwork. I immediately wrote a letter to the president of the International Olympic Committee, telling him my idea. Although I used the wrong address, I soon received a personal reply from him. He said that he found my idea interesting and in perfect alignment with the principles of the Olympic movement. He said he would recommend my idea to the host country (South Korea), but that they would have to make the final decision. To my disappointment, they decided not to do it.

I've noticed that when I have a goal that is primarily for my own benefit, I am less resourceful than when I have a dream that includes others. Spirit seemed to keep pushing me to do everything I could to turn my dream into a reality. I persevered. After the Koreans failed to do what I began calling the "Hope Heard 'Round the World," I wrote letters to the Barcelona Olympic Committee. After initial enthusiasm for the idea, they too failed to do it. For the 1996 Olympics in Atlanta, I decided to pull out all the stops. I began to market my dream fully.

As I relentlessly shared my vision with others, some high-level individuals became inspired to offer their help. A man who knew Jimmy Carter offered to tell him about the idea. A woman who knew Hillary Clinton offered to tell her about it. I even got a letter through to Ted Turner. Soon, I had a whole squadron of VIPs pressuring the one man who would make the decision about this event. When I was on the *Oprah* show, I gave Oprah a letter asking her to lend support for this event. As I watched the opening ceremonies for the Atlanta games, I didn't know if it was going to happen or not. It never did. I was once again disappointed, but I became determined to make it happen for the 2000 Olympic Games.

Two weeks later, when I didn't expect it, my dream came true. As I watched the closing ceremonies in Atlanta, I was surprised to hear the president of the Olympic committee, Mr. Samaranch, announce that there would be a time for all of us to unite in a moment of silence. With billions of people participating, the 30 seconds of silence was followed by Stevie Wonder leading the world in the singing of John Lennon's song, "Imagine." After the song, kids from every country on Earth joined together on the Olympic lawn and sang a song called "The Power to Live the Dream." There was hardly a dry eye in the stadium, and as I watched the event on TV, I felt a hurricane of loving energy descend upon me. It was truly amazing.

Having the "Hope Heard 'Round the World" happen taught me many things. First, I learned that people can accomplish anything if they persevere and enlist the right individuals. I also realized how beautiful it is to "market" a dream that you feel totally passionate about. When people volunteered to help me, it often brought tears to my eyes. As I worked on making the event happen, I felt God's loving hands infusing me with energy despite eight years of disappointments. Finally, I learned that marketing something you fully believe in is totally different from trying to *sell* something.

When people come across the word *marketing*, they rarely get excited. Yet, by understanding the principles of what I call "integrity marketing," you can make your dreams come true— and have a great time doing it. The first principle of marketing with integrity is to market something you truly believe in. To passionately believe in something, it is necessary to know that what you're marketing will strongly benefit others. The more you truly know this, the easier it is to be fully passionate about it. I was able to "sell" the "Hope Heard 'Round the World" because I fully believed it would be of service to the world as a whole. When I spoke to others about my idea, they became inspired because they sensed my enthusiasm and pure intent.

When marketing your dream, your services, or your product, you need to know that what you're "selling" will be of much greater benefit to your "customers" than the price they will have to pay. For example, most of us would have a hard time marketing a seminar that lacked any really useful information. Yet, it would be easy to market a seminar that *guaranteed* to help people make an extra $5,000 in income in just one month—if you *really* believed it could deliver the goods and improve people's lives.

How do you find a cause or something to market that you really believe in? Begin by being on the lookout for such things. Follow any thread of an idea or product that you think could really benefit a lot of people. Some of the leads you follow will take you nowhere, but if you follow enough of them, you'll finally find the magic carpet you've been looking for. Consider asking Spirit the question, "How can I use the gifts I've been given to serve people?" Most of the ideas and projects I've passionately pursued came to me as a result of asking that question. Sometimes the answer did not come right away. Yet, as I kept asking, it seems that an answer has always become clear to me during the course of my life.

A second principle of integrity marketing is to be willing to find out what others truly want, and to become committed to providing it for them. Although I had long heard the business maxim, "Find a need and fill it," it never got me excited until I realized that filling other's needs is simply another way of saying, "Give selfless service." When you can meet someone's need and pursue your passion at the same time, then you really have a powerful combination. Since I feel passionate about meditation, I figured I would try to come up with a meditation tape that people would really love. To better serve others, before I created the tape I asked dozens of people why they didn't regularly meditate. I learned that most individuals don't meditate regularly because they feel they don't have enough time, or they find it too boring. Therefore, I became committed to making a short tape that would provide an immediate and profound experience.

After a year of trial and error exploring various methods, I finally created *The Ten-Minute Pure Love Meditation Experience.* In the seminars I lead, I've found that about 60 percent of the audience are moved to tears of love while listening to this ten-minute tape. It is now my bestselling product! I get excited talking to people about it. I don't feel like I'm selling them something, but rather I feel that I am giving them hundreds of dollars' worth of methods and experience—while asking for only $10 from them. It's a win-win situation. I found what others wanted, and I gave it to them in a way they can appreciate.

A third principle of integrity marketing is to recognize the value of people. Whatever your financial, personal, or spiritual dreams, they cannot be fulfilled without truly caring for others. If you own a store, your job is to make people feel good about doing business with you. Besides offering them products or services that are useful, you can make them feel valued in other ways. Just as in intimate relationships, little things can make a big difference. A nice smile, a kind word, or simply a sincere desire to be of help can go a long way in making your business stand out above the rest.

I used to go to a copy shop that was near where I lived, but the attitude of the employees toward the customers was always very poor. Although it was a bit out of my way, one day I decided to go to another copy shop. The owner greeted me with a warm smile—as if he were really happy to see me. I told him what I needed copied and asked him when I could pick it up. To my surprise he said, "I'll do it right now—it'll only take a few minutes." As he copied my material, he started up a friendly conversation with me and seemed truly interested in what I was writing. As I paid for the copies, he asked me if I would like some free memo pads to use as scrap paper. Indeed, I needed some memo pads, and he gave me about a dozen of them. He asked me if I wanted a box or help carrying my materials out to my car. I felt like royalty. The man made a customer for life.

In business, there's an obscure term called *the marginal net worth per customer.* In essence, this term refers to the amount of money you stand to make from a single customer over the life of your business. To figure this out accurately, you need to also include the amount of money you might receive from all the referred business you receive from a given customer. In the case of the copy shop and me, I once figured that I have spent about $1,200 a year at this establishment, of which about $1,000 ends up being the owner's profit. Over the last seven years, that means he's made roughly $7,000 profit from me. But the story doesn't end there. I've told at least 20 people about this copy shop, and about half of them have become loyal customers. If they spend the same amount as I do, that means the shop has ultimately made $70,000 from having me as a customer over the past seven years! That's a nice reward for just a few minutes of good service.

How much is each customer worth to *you?* Do you treat the people you do business with as if they were worth a million dollars, or like they're just ordinary customers? Figuring out the marginal net worth of each customer you do business with can be an eye-opening experience. It can help you see that each satisfied patron can have a major impact on your financial life. Yet, customers know when you're just being courteous to make an extra buck and when you're being helpful because you really care about people. It's nice to know that purity of heart can result in more business and money.

In my work as a psychotherapist, at first I was a bit hesitant to show people how much I cared about them. I thought they might think I was weird. Yet, as I've overcome my fears, I've developed deeper relationships with my clients, and I've received more referrals. In this often apathetic world, people like to do business with caring people. And even if it *didn't* lead to more business, showing people that you appreciate them just makes work more meaningful and pleasant.

A fourth aspect of marketing with integrity is to understand the potential power of commitment. If you have a dream that you really believe in, then you need to be willing to persevere until it becomes a reality. As I've come to know many successful authors and entrepreneurs, I've seen that just about all of them share the trait of being fully committed to whatever they are marketing. It's almost as if they won't take no for an answer. It's not that they're pushy—they just believe so much in what they're doing that they persist despite the many trials they inevitably encounter.

People sometimes ask me how I managed to interview 40 of the best-known spiritual leaders in the world for my book *Bridges to Heaven*. I tell them that I deeply believed in the value of the project and that I was completely committed to making it happen. Only when I received a definite no from someone would I give up. For some people, that meant that I sent them over 20 letters. After sending author/spiritual guru Ram Dass multiple letters (and receiving no reply), he finally called me on the phone. In a friendly tone he said, "Because I get so many requests for interviews, I've decided I just won't do them anymore. However, I've never seen anyone quite as persistent as you. The only reason I'm calling is to see if you're on a mission from God, or if you're a complete lunatic." When I convinced him that I was not the latter, he decided to grant me the interview.

In both the world of business and spirit, there are hundreds of stories of people who would not take no for an answer. Colonel Sanders tried to sell his chicken recipe to 1,009 restaurants before he received his first yes. The *Chicken Soup for the Soul* book was turned down by every major publisher before it went on to sell many millions of copies. Zen master Hui-ko was repeatedly turned away by his teacher, Bodhidharma, the founder of Zen Buddhism. Finally, in a last-ditch effort to show his Zen master that he was a serious disciple, Hui-ko cut off his arm and gave it to Bodhidarma. That's when he was finally accepted as a student. Hopefully, you won't have to show your level of commitment the way Hui-ko did. Yet, Spirit knows when we're really committed to helping people—versus when we are not. I believe that the greater the level of our commitment, the more Spirit is compelled to help us out.

The final principle of integrity marketing is the ability to use one's intuition as the basis for making important business decisions. Rationality, analysis, and competence in one's field all have their limitations. Even after gathering a mountain of information, stockbrokers don't really have any idea which stocks will go up or down. Despite the fact that knowledge and expertise are helpful in any business, no one can consistently state what will do well and what won't. Therefore, successful business people are not afraid to use their intuition as an aid in making important decisions. They know that intuition, hunches, and gut feelings can sometimes be more important than market research, past experience, or rational analysis.

A study was done several years ago in which two groups of executives were given ESP tests. The first group were involved in businesses that were doing particularly well. They were highly regarded in their field of expertise because they seemed to make a lot of the right moves. The second group of executives worked for businesses that were in a slump. In their executive roles, they had made decisions that led to poorer sales and profits. When these two groups were given ESP tests, the successful executives scored 500 percent better than their less successful counterparts. The conclusion the authors of this study made was that successful business people use psychic abilities without even knowing it.

Previously, I discussed ways you can learn to better tap into your own intuitive abilities. Yet, the most important step is to simply practice. Whenever you're facing an important business or marketing decision, ask yourself, "What is my gut feeling about what's right to do here?" Notice when your intuition later ends up being right and when it ends up being wrong. Over time, you may notice subtle clues as to when it's critical to listen to the still, small voice within.

A few years back, I was on a national TV talk show speaking about my video on relationships. While on the show, they allowed me to tell viewers the 800 number for ordering the video. I ended up selling over $25,000 worth of videos. About nine months later, the company who had taken all those calls asked me if I still needed my 800 number. The number was costing me about $50 a month to keep, and I had no one ordering the video anymore through that phone number. I decided to cancel it, despite the fact that my gut feeling was to keep it. My mind kept saying, "There's no reason to keep this number. Save the money."

About a month later, I was at home on Sunday night reading a book. A small voice inside was prompting me to turn on the TV. I normally watch very little TV, but I relented. When I turned it on, I saw myself on the talk show I had done ten months earlier! I felt a wave of panic as I realized I was going to give out a disconnected 800 number to a national audience in about ten minutes. I raced to the phone and called the company who had previously taken the video orders. Luckily, there was someone at the office to answer the phone. It took me about eight minutes to clarify my situation to them. I asked them if they could *immediately* hook up my old 800 number. Five seconds before I said the number on TV, they got it hooked up. That night I received another $25,000 worth of orders for my video. I made a lot of money, but more important, I learned that it can pay to listen to one's intuition.

In the world of business, we are constantly faced with decisions. What product should we sell, what ad should we run, what service should we focus on? Gathering as much information as possible is necessary to the success of any business. Yet, as spiritual beings, we need to respect both the analytical and intuitive sides of our nature. By gathering rational information *and* listening to the "still, small voice" within, we can improve our chances of success. As one becomes better at applying the principles of integrity marketing, it's possible to do a lot of honorable work in the world—and have a good time doing it.

❧ ❧ ❧

REAL WEALTH REMINDERS

1. By understanding the five principles of "integrity marketing," you can make your dreams come true—and have a great time doing it. The first principle of marketing with integrity is to sell something you truly believe in.

2. The second, third, and fourth principles of integrity marketing are: find out what others want and become committed to providing it for them, recognize and indicate the value you have for each customer and person you work for, and understand the power of perseverance.

3. The final principle for marketing your dreams is to use your intuition, in collaboration with your rational mind, as the basis for making important decisions. To do so, get in the habit of asking yourself, "What's my gut feeling about what is right to do in this situation?"

PART THREE

From Goal to Soul

CHAPTER TEN

TITHING AND OTHER EXPERIMENTS

"Money is like an arm or a leg—use it or lose it."
— Henry Ford

In the last 100 years, science has dramatically changed how we think and live. Why? Because it works. Through the scientific method, we've learned valuable lessons about how the Universe operates, and we've translated those insights into greater techno-logical abilities. Unfortunately, we can't say the same thing about spirituality. Instead of building on what others have learned (as science has), the fields of religion and spirituality have mostly bickered about whose approach to God is right or wrong. In the last 5,000 years, it could be said that the "science" of knowing God has not advanced much on a global scale. It's time for this to change.

Science has progressed rapidly because it uses experiments to verify or disprove certain principles. In a similar way, you and I can test things out in order to learn valuable ways of integrating our financial and spiritual lives. In the context I'm using, an "experiment" is a specific thing you try for a period of time in order to see what effect it has on your spiritual and/or financial life. For example, you could try tithing (giving away 10 percent of your income) for a predetermined period of time. As in any scientific procedure, when doing a tithing experiment, you'll get the greatest benefit if you carefully notice the results of your new behavior. If you notice that over a six-month period of tithing, your income dramatically increases, you feel more loving, and you feel better about yourself, then you could say that your experiment indicated that tithing "works" for you. On the other hand, if you notice that tithing leads to even more money worries, then you'd be smart to try a different way to contribute to others.

Experiments can help people learn new things and try new behaviors that they might otherwise never try. It's a lot less frightening to try tithing for a single month than it is to decide to tithe for the rest of your life. Yet, if your month-long trial run proves promising, it wouldn't be very hard to try a long-term tithing commitment.

When it comes to finances, most people are hesitant to put their money where their soul is. They play the money game strictly by the rules of logic—rather than by spiritual principles. By conducting short-term money experiments, we can gradually become free of our prison of logic and rationality. When our tests are "successful"—meaning that they lead to more peace, money, or contribution—we expand. When our efforts lead to less peace, money, or contribution, we learn valuable lessons.

To create your own experiment, you don't need an expensive lab. All you need is a desire to learn. Whatever you try, you should do it long enough so that you really learn what you want to know, and briefly enough so that you can fully commit to it. For instance, a few years ago I became motivated to doing nice things for strangers after I heard an inspiring sermon. Rather than simply being inspired for a day, I decided to do an experiment for a full month to see what effect it would have on my life. If, after a month of being kind to strangers, I felt spiritually uplifted, then I'd continue. If my month-long trial proved to be unfulfilling or a waste of valuable time, I would have learned a valuable lesson.

The first thing I did during my month-long experiment was buy about $25 worth of ice cream and go to the local beach with a sign that read "Free Ice Cream." I set up a little table and my sign in a crowded part of the beach, and braced myself for the rush of people to my ice cream stand. I was disappointed. Although many people gave me curious looks, no one came for a full 15 minutes. Finally, as my ice cream began to melt, a cute little six-year old girl walked up and asked me in a shy voice, "How much is your free ice cream?" I told her that if she gave me a smile, I'd give her a double scoop for nothing. She squealed with delight. When watchful parents saw that the little girl didn't die from food poisoning, the mass pilgrimage to my holy ice cream stand began.

As I scooped up smile after smile for wide-eyed kids, many suspicious parents began asking me why I was giving away free ice cream. I told them, "I like to do nice things for people because it makes me feel good." That seemed to quell their suspicions. While I scooped up ice cream for their kids, several of the parents asked me what I did for a living. When I told them I was a psychotherapist, four people asked me for my business card. Since I was at the beach to give away ice cream, I didn't have my card, but I told them that my number was in the phone book. It ends up that three of the people I met that day called for appointments. Months later I added up all the money I made from the appointments I had with these three people, and it totaled over $1,000. That's a pretty decent reward for having a good time, making a lot of people happy, and spending only $25 on ice cream!

After a month of randomly doing kind things for people, I realized that I felt better about myself and more aligned with Spirit. I was also making more money due to business I picked up from treating people with more kindness and respect. Therefore, I decided to be kind to strangers as a way of life. By writing in my journal periodically throughout my initial "kindness experiment," I had proof that acting this way was beneficial to me (as well as others). This inspired me to look into the possibility of giving away 10 percent of my income. Although I had read that tithing can be a very beneficial practice, I was always too cheap to try it out. Yet, the success of my kindness experiment suggested that I might be able to find a way to tithe that did not overwhelm me.

A New Way to Tithe

Traditionally, tithing has been the practice of giving away 10 percent of one's income to a religious organization, such as a church or synagogue. A survey of my friends and family indicated that virtually none of them gave away 10 percent of their income to the spiritual organizations they were affiliated with. Nor did I. In trying to understand why this was the case, I realized that several factors prevented my friends and me from tithing. First of all, we were cheap. Ten percent is a large amount of money, and most of us didn't feel we could afford to give away that much of our income. Second, we didn't see how giving away 10 percent of our income would be worth the price that we were paying. And finally, many of my friends didn't believe that their church or temple needed or deserved 10 percent—especially when there were so many other causes to support.

With this information in mind, I decided to look for a new way to tithe that might help people consistently contribute to others—without adding additional anxiety to their own lives. After trying various methods, I came upon a formula that has worked quite well. In essence, I've decided that 10 percent of what I make is not my personal money, but rather it's "God's money." I have a separate account for this money, and 10 percent of everything I make goes into this account. Once a month, I spend time getting quiet inside, and then I ask for guidance about who or where this money should go. Oftentimes I get a clear intuitive sense of where "God's money" should go, and how much should go there. Since this money is in a different account and is not really "mine," it's easy to surrender my control and simply listen for what would be best to do with it. If I don't receive a clear message, I just allow the money to sit in the account until the next time I ask.

Since God ultimately wants me to experience more peace and love, I sometimes ask Spirit if I can dip into the "God's money" account for a purpose that benefits me. For example, recently I had several clients who didn't pay me, and I was feeling resentful, hurt, and anxious. In a moment of quiet meditation, I asked if it was okay to receive the money I was owed from my tithing account. The answer I received was yes. Receiving this money (from my tithing account) helped me feel at peace. I quickly let go of the anger I'd been feeling toward the clients who hadn't paid me. Previously, I used to be greatly bothered by clients who didn't pay their bills. Yet now I can ask if I can be charitable toward myself when I've been wronged, and most of the time I get the message that it's okay.

While doing this "loose" form of tithing may seem less than totally pure, it has allowed me to consistently give to others while avoiding becoming anxious about money. Since I now know that 10 percent of the money I make isn't mine, I feel more at ease giving money away to worthy people and causes. It's resulted in a freer, more relaxed feeling about money. It has also led to me being more generous. Once each month, or whenever I notice I have several hundred dollars in my tithing account, I'll ask "How can I use this money to bring more joy and healing into the world?" I receive different answers each time I ask. Sometimes I'll feel a desire to give money to a friend in need—or simply give someone a present. Other times I'll write a check to a charity that I feel does important work. Because I am not writing a check from "my" account, I can give this money away with a true feeling of service. If this way of tithing seems like it might work for you, I suggest that you try it as an experiment and see how it feels.

The Budget Experiment

I've always hated the idea of being on a budget. However, when I realized how much I spend eating out each month, I decided to try a one-month budget experiment. During this month, I decided I could only spend $100 on eating out. Since at the time I was spending about $200 per month at restaurants, my experiment required that I become creative. For me, an experiment is like a game you play with yourself. Because I hate to cook, I had to look for creative ways to save money—without cooking at home all the time. The first thing I did was call up some friends to see if they would have me over for dinner. They were happy to do so. Next, I asked my partner to cook for me more often, and in exchange I promised to give her more massages. Third, I learned to cook a new dish at home that was satisfying and didn't cost much. And last, I skipped dinner a couple of times during the month to save time and money.

The results of my one-month budget experiment were incredibly positive. I lost four pounds, saved over $120, and became closer to my partner and several friends. Since then, I have not stayed on a food budget, but because I'm more aware of my various options, I have ended up spending less than before. I no longer mechanically go to restaurants whenever I'm hungry. Sometimes I cook one of the new dishes I've learned to prepare, and sometimes I ask my partner or a friend to cook for me. Creating your own budget experiment can be an effective and fun way to try new behaviors and find hidden ways of saving money.

Overcoming-Worry Experiments

Do you needlessly worry about money and work? Many people do. Despite the fact that worrying about money is so common, few people have studied how to overcome this useless waste of energy. In the New Testament, Jesus told his disciples, "And do not set your heart on what you will eat or drink; do not worry about it. For the pagan world runs after all such things, and your Father knows that you need them. But seek his kingdom, and these things will be given to you as well." Easier said than done. Unfortunately, Jesus didn't provide specific instruction as to *how* we can stop our needless worrying. That part of the formula we have to figure out for ourselves.

If we have a clear-cut goal to worry less about money and work, it's possible to design experiments that can help us achieve this goal. I have created several such experiments, and some have been particularly effective in reducing the time and energy I spend thinking about financial concerns. The first thing I found helpful was my "live on nothing" experiment. For eight weeks I set out to see if I could live on no money at all. Growing up in an upper-middle-class family, money was always available. Yet, I had a fear of someday having my "safety net" stripped away and being left destitute. I figured the best way out of a fear was to go through it. Therefore, I decided to travel around the United States without any money at all. I loaded up a backpack and set out to hitchhike across the country with only a quarter in my pocket—and a Visa card in case of an emergency.

When I tell this story in my *Real Wealth* seminars, people are amazed that I could survive. Actually, it was quite easy. I would simply go into small towns and knock on people's doors and explain to them what I was doing. Fully 90 percent of the people whom I asked for help allowed me to sleep in their yard or home and gave me free food to eat. Some people offered me several meals and even gave me money. I had a terrific time. Not only did

I see that I could be fine without any money, but it also restored my faith in humanity. Although you may not be in a position to try this experiment, it's nice to know that it's possible to survive on other people's generosity. My experience of living without money helped me realize that I need not ever worry about my survival.

Although I'm no longer concerned about surviving in the material world, occasionally I still feel uneasy about money-related concerns. In order to alleviate this worrying even more, I have tried many methods. What works for me may not be what works for you, so I encourage you to try your own experiment. Yet, by describing what has worked for me, you will at least get a couple of ideas that are worth exploring. First, whenever I notice that I'm spending needless time thinking about money-related matters, I tell myself that I'll "think about it on Sunday." Saying this helps me release these thoughts in the present. At the same time, it reassures me that if I need to attend to a certain financial matter, I'll be able to do so on that day.

Why Sunday? For me, Sunday afternoon is a good time to reflect. At precisely 3:00 P.M. until 3:30 P.M., I allow myself to worry about my finances all I desire. Occasionally I really *do* have something I need to think about, and devoting a specific, focused time to ruminating about it is quite helpful. Of course, most of the time I don't remember what I was worrying about during the previous week. If I can't remember what I was concerned about, I figure that it probably wasn't very important—so I just let it go. By putting off my worry until Sunday, I manage to avoid thinking a lot of unnecessary thoughts. It's really worked great.

Once you're turned on to the idea of doing experiments, you'll find it easier to begin implementing financial advice you used to be too lazy to try. For example, I used to be too lazy to even think of budgeting, yet I *was* willing to do a one-month budgeting experiment. Once you see that something works, it's not that hard to keep doing it. Yet, I should warn you that some things clearly won't work for you. Each person is different, so it makes sense that each person needs to handle his or her finances in a unique way. Even though most financial experts speak of the benefits of tithing, budgeting, and paying yourself first, if it doesn't work for you, then it doesn't work. In my own case, I have often read about the many advantages of paying yourself first (10 percent off the top to invest), but it never worked for me. Therefore, I don't do it, and have instead explored other ways to invest. Yet, it may work beautifully for you. Why don't you try it—as an experiment?

Business Experiments

If you're a business owner, or have some clout at the company you work for, you can suggest conducting experiments that may benefit a lot of people. The business world needs fearless leaders who are willing to merge spiritual principles into the bottom line. Businesses such as Ben and Jerry's ice cream or Anita Rodick's Body Shops have shown that doing good can lead to an even better bottom line. Yet, even presidents of corporations are now realizing that there is more to life than making a profit. Companies who go for short-term gains over caring for their employees almost always end up paying for it. As someone with influence, you may be able to influence the short-sighted corporate culture that now dominates American business.

There are many ways to help a business or a company become more "spiritually aligned." For one thing, you can help create an atmosphere of openness and mutual respect. At many companies, there is an "us against them" mentality within the ranks. On the other hand, at more "spiritually evolved" companies, there is a "we're all in this together" feeling. A work environment that includes kindness, openness, and agreed-upon common goals is much more likely to exist long term than those that are stress factories.

If you're in a position of power, you may even try creating a companywide mission statement, or choosing a favorite charity in which to give a percentage of your profits. In working with businesses and CEOs, I've seen that clarity of purpose and an atmosphere that fosters creativity and cooperation is priceless. When employees feel cared for and part of a larger purpose, their productivity goes up and their absenteeism goes down. Companies are finding that the management styles of past decades no longer work so well in today's business climate. The CEOs and business owners who are willing to experiment with more "human" ways of doing things will likely enjoy less stress and more wealth.

REAL WEALTH REMINDERS

1. A money "experiment" is a specific thing you do for a period of time in order to try new behaviors and learn new things. For example, you can try tithing for a brief time to see what effect it has on your spiritual and/or financial life. If your experiment leads to more peace, money, or a greater sense of contribution, then it would be a good idea to continue it.

2. In order to find ways of handling money and work that are best for you, you can try various budgeting, investing, and nonworrying experiments. By noticing the results of your experiments, you can quickly grow wiser and more competent at handling money.

3. If you're a business owner, you can conduct experiments that may benefit a lot of people. Creating an atmosphere of openness, a companywide mission statement, or giving a percentage of your profits to charity are examples of worthy attempts to integrate spiritual principles into one's business.

CHAPTER ELEVEN

BALANCING WORK AND SPIRIT

"It is easier for a camel to pass through the eye of a needle than for a rich man to enter the kingdom of Heaven."
— Jesus of Nazareth

The above quote does not exactly motivate a person to pursue wealth. Jesus' words serve as a powerful reminder that successfully juggling the world of money, work, and spirit is quite a chore. When Jesus' disciples heard him say these words, they asked, "Who then can be saved?" Jesus reportedly looked at them and said, "With man this is impossible, but with God all things are possible." All things are indeed possible with God's assistance, but it sure helps if we do our part and learn how to help God help us. In this chapter, we'll look at some final ideas and methods to help you balance money, work, and spirit more effectively.

In chapter 2, I discussed financial traps that people fall into that interfere with their spiritual connection. For each of these five "lower" ways of using money, I delineated "higher" ways to make use of one's money. Now, I'd like to discuss a few ways in which people can allow success in their *careers* to interfere with their spirituality, as well as ways to avoid such traps.

For starters, one of the biggest success traps is the desire to accumulate increasing amounts of power. Almost all high-level business people I've worked with have said that power is like an addictive drug. People crave it when it's within their grasp, and experience withdrawal symptoms when they lose it. To make matters worse, it often conceals its true identity by cloaking itself in the desire to do noble deeds. Once one has achieved a high-level position, the temptation to use power (whether for "good" or "bad") is enormous. I've known many clients who have had a desire to use their power to help others and have seemingly succeeded in manifesting worthy things. Yet, their efforts were often at the price of their own health, relationships, and spiritual peace of mind.

The question we need to consider is: "How can we exercise the power granted to us in a way that serves both ourselves and others?" If we serve our own purposes too much, we become selfish and greedy. If we serve others too much, we can become burned out. I believe that the more influence we have, the more we need to seek God's guidance to know how best to use that authority. The problem with power is that we can soon get lost thinking that WE are the force that makes things happen. Spirituality, on the other hand, is largely the experience of surrendering our will to the will of God. Unless we are willing to surrender the power we've been given to the will of Spirit, the authority we've accumulated can serve to cut us off from God.

In my own life, I have tried to develop a "hot and cold detector" to inform me when I'm using power correctly—and when I am not. When I feel stressed, burned out, or easily annoyed, I sense I am getting "cooler," *even* if I'm accomplishing a lot. When I feel loving, joyful, and humble while exerting power, I sense I'm getting "warmer." Over time I've noticed that certain situations almost always make me "lose it"—meaning that I get trapped in the desire to exert MY will. However, there are also situations in which I *have* been able to get things done and feel loving and humble. I believe that a good "hot and cold detector"—which is basically self-honesty—can keep people from getting completely lost in the world of power. Yet, you must be careful and aware. The desire for power can sneak up on you and quickly overtake your higher instincts.

Closely related to the desire for power is the problem of getting caught up in the momentum of success. Like a snowball gathering mass as it speeds down a hill, "success momentum" can flatten your spiritual aspirations like a pancake. When things are going well in your career, it's easy to become so lost in it that the world of Spirit pales in comparison. If you are in a position of very high-level success, people start to treat you as if *you* (your ego) were God. Of course, the problem here is that your ego can begin to take all the credit, and you can end up becoming an arrogant, self-absorbed, and greedy executive.

To counteract the problem of success momentum, it can be helpful to take periodic vacations away from your world of work. In the last three years, I've made a vow to myself to get out of town for at least three days every eight weeks. During these three days, I let go of work completely. If possible, I spend my time in nature, slowing down the momentum that has been created in my life. While camping out among soaring redwood trees or sleeping underneath a vast desert sky, my rightful (small) place in the Universe can once again be established. I'm always amazed at how, even after just one day away from work, my perspective of what's important is radically altered. "Getting away from it all" in a natural setting can truly heal the soul.

When people become successful in their work, there is a tendency to focus on it to the detriment of other areas of their life. Yet, spiritual growth comes from facing our weaknesses, not our strengths. Basically, our lives are only as good as the worst thing in them. For example, if you're a zillionaire, but you've never been good at close relationships, then you'll likely feel a profound emptiness—despite the fact that you have all the money you'll ever need. To truly be happy, we have to focus on improving the areas of our lives that don't work so well. Such effort leads to a balanced, harmonious life. While achieving balance is always difficult, it can be made even harder when one's career is progressing at full speed.

When I counsel successful businessmen and women, I encourage them to set firm limits as to how much time they will spend at work. I suggest they schedule frequent mini-vacations out of town. Most important, I encourage them to look at the other areas of their lives, become aware of what is not working so well, and spend time attending to those needs. Although this is initially difficult to do when work is so easy and rewarding, it creates long-term success, harmony, and happiness. Isn't that what the goal was, anyway?

As an additional way to help my clients maintain balance in their lives, I give them a list of questions they can periodically ask themselves. I've listed these questions below. I think it's helpful to take a few minutes every week to evaluate how things are going in one's life and make appropriate adjustments when necessary. Although it's common to evaluate our lives on an annual basis, for example, around New Year's, I don't think that's enough. By asking yourself the following seven questions on a weekly basis, you can better redirect your energy in beneficial ways before a major problem is created.

Questions for Self-Evaluation

1. What problem or situation am I not properly attending to or avoiding in my life?

2. What can I do to begin to better handle this situation?

3. What area of my life (health, relationships, spirituality, career and finances, etc.) is most lacking?

4. What are a couple of small things I can do to make this area of my life just a little bit better?

5. What do I need to know (or do) to experience even more peace and love in my life?

6. Is there anything I'm doing that is hurting myself, other people, or steering me off course?

7. How can I use the gifts I've been given to better serve people?

These questions are best answered after you've spent some time getting quiet inside. Although they can be answered from your intellect, they can also be answered from a deep, intuitive place within you. Many people find it helpful to write the answers they get in a journal and to immediately schedule items that relate to the answers received. If the answers you receive are hard to put into practice, then consider writing a contract (from chapter 8) that includes the new behaviors. In my own contract, I have included two "date nights" with my girlfriend, and at least one walk in nature every week. Even though I love to engage in both of those activities, I used to get caught up in business and forget such things. Not anymore. Answering the seven questions above and having a contract to keep my life in balance has had a dramatic effect on the quality of my life.

Cycles of Life

Fulfillment is best achieved by creating a life that maintains a healthy balance between one's work and time spent on spiritual, personal, and family activities. Yet, there is another model for success that has a long-standing history and should be mentioned here. In cultures such as India, people were traditionally expected to fully pursue *one* specific area of life at a time. For example, between the ages of 25 and 50, men were encouraged to make as much money as they possibly could for their families and their retirement. Once they fulfilled their family's financial needs, they were to become "full-time" spiritual seekers. Ideally, they would leave their families and possessions behind and wander the country as holy men.

In the Western world, we don't have an abundance of elderly, wandering holy men or women rambling the countryside. However, we do have the cultural dream of early retirement. As in India, we are encouraged to work hard during certain years of our lives so we can have plenty of free time when we're older. But what is it we're supposed to do when we're retired? In India, people are encouraged to renounce the material world so they can fully embrace their soul. Things are just slightly different in the West. After one is freed from financial needs, our culture encourages people to indulge their desires as much as money will allow.

In many spiritual traditions, part of the teaching is that the best time to pursue spiritual "work" is when one is older. When we're older, we're hopefully a bit wiser. We know that the next relationship or paycheck is not going to be the answer to all our dreams. We become aware that life is short, filled with difficulty, and that time steals our health and loved ones from us. It's a perfect time to become more devoted to seeking one's spiritual essence. Yet, there are challenges. After a life filled with "busy"ness and worldly success, it can be extremely difficult to dive within. I've seen many people hold on to the idea that, once they retire, they'll become more devoted to their soul. Unfortunately, I've rarely seen people *do* it. If your hope is to fully embrace Spirit once you've retired, it might be wise to lay a good foundation for that pursuit while you're still making a living. Then, when you're freed from the need to work, you'll be better prepared to pursue your inner dream.

I knew a man named Brian who, upon saving enough money to live for a year, decided to take a year off. Brian was burned out from 70 hour weeks as an attorney. He wanted to see what would happen if he was free to pursue his spiritual aspirations. He soon became bored. Brian found that with so much time on his hands, it was hard to be disciplined in his spiritual life. After a month, he decided to visit the law firm he used to work for. While at the firm, he heard about a case that involved a nonprofit environmental group suing a major corporation. The other attorneys didn't want to take the case because they didn't think they'd win. Although Brian would only be paid on a contingency basis (that is, only if he won the case), he found the work fascinating and began looking into it in greater depth.

To avoid getting too caught up in the new case, Brian decided to live by a simple rule during his one-year sabbatical: He would only work on the case if it were truly the thing he most wanted to do in that moment. Since his life was now less stressful and more balanced, he got a lot done—even though he was only working a few hours a week. The lawsuit took several months, but Brian and the group he represented finally won the case. In an ironic turn of events, Brian ended up making more money during his "year off" than he had at any time previously.

As the example with Brian shows, balancing the various aspects of one's life can sometimes lead to making more money. Yet, even when it doesn't, it can immediately lead to a life of greater ease and harmony. If you find yourself with enough money to take some time off, you might try what Brian did. Think of yourself as "semiretired," only pursuing work and money when you have an inner calling to do so. For most people, "full-time" retirement isn't all it's cracked up to be. As I mentioned earlier in this book, men who retire have a life expectancy of only 67 years, whereas men who continue to work report they are happier and tend to live to be 75 or more. Once you have some money saved, you're in an excellent position to experiment with doing work you enjoy, and only working when you desire. Once you find a career that is truly fulfilling, it means you never have to "work" for a living. You can reach the true ideal—making a lot of money while pursuing your passion.

❧ ❧ ❧

Real Wealth Reminders

1. Career success can sometimes interfere with a person creating a balanced, spiritual life. Two particular "success traps" to be wary of are the desire to accumulate power and the tendency to get caught up in the momentum of success.

2. To create a balanced life, several things can be of enormous help. For example, asking specific questions to evaluate how your life is going can quickly get you on track when you've veered off course. In addition, frequent mini-vacations, intense self-honesty, and writing contracts with yourself can also be very useful.

3. Rather than trying to retire early, it might be a good idea to take some time off from your job and use your extra money to pursue work that is highly rewarding. If you can make money doing work you enjoy, then you can more easily create a life of balance, purpose, and real wealth.

AFTERWORD

Many spiritual seekers live double lives. When it comes to money and work, they live by the principles of logic, efficiency, and conformity. Yet, when it comes to the rest of their lives, they try to live by spiritual principles and guidance. Unfortunately, the world's great spiritual traditions have had little to say about how to make a 40-hour work week, a mortgage, and car payments part of one's spiritual path. In this book, you've been given a variety of ways to integrate spiritual principles into your career and financial lives. Now is the time to act on what you've learned. In the Bible it says, "Faith by itself, if it is not accompanied by action, is dead." In a similar way, I believe that knowledge, if not soon acted upon, dies.

St. Francis once said, "The measure of a person's knowledge is the actions they take." Everyone can "be spiritual" in church or when they're doing their particular spiritual practice. The true test of our spiritual maturity is whether we can live by our higher principles while active in the material world. To do so takes courage, faith, and the right knowledge. The information you need to spiritually navigate through the business world exists in three places. First, it exists in this book. As you face particular challenges, I suggest you reread the chapters that apply to your current situation. I think you'll find the techniques and ideas to be of great practical help when you find yourself in uncharted waters.

A second place to turn for help in "spiritualizing" your financial life is to friends who have a similar intention as you. In a culture that does not advocate the blending of money, work, and spirit, people need all the help they can get. I encourage you to talk with your friends about this subject and tell them about this book. The more you do so, the easier it will be to make these concepts ongoing priorities in your life. I am fortunate to have many friends with whom I've been able to share ideas and concerns, and gain valuable feedback from. With the mutual support we provide for each other, it has been easier to overcome many of the challenges that result from blending one's spiritual and financial lives.

A third and final place to turn for support is in your relationship with Spirit. I believe that God wants us to release our fears and bring the light of awareness to all our endeavors. As I look back over the last ten years, I can see God's loving hands teaching me through my various jobs and financial dealings. If you sincerely look for the lessons and listen for God's guidance, it will surely be there. The Creator *can* help guide us through the "mundane" activities of our lives. As we build our bridge between the material world and spirit, our lives are transformed. We become more peaceful, more loving, and better able to contribute to others. A spiritual approach to money and work eventually leads to the real wealth we all truly desire.

RECOMMENDED RESOURCES

BOOKS

The Abundance Book, by John Randolph Price
Creating Money, by Sonya Roman
Do What You Love, the Money Will Follow, by Marsha Sinetar
Gratitude: A Way of Life, by Louise Hay
The Trick to Money Is Having Some, by Stuart Wilde

AUDIOS

Meditations for Manifesting, by Dr. Wayne W. Dyer
Real Wealth One-Day Seminar, by Jonathan Robinson

ORGANIZATIONS

Conscious Business Alliance
4243 Grimes Ave. South
Edina, MN 55416
(612) 925-5995

Businesses for Social Responsibility
1850 M St.
Washington, D.C. 20036
(202) 842-5400

ABOUT JONATHAN ROBINSON

Jonathan Robinson is a professional speaker, psychotherapist, and author who lives in Santa Barbara, California. He specializes in providing businesses with practical tools that can immediately be used to increase their level of productivity, profitability, creativity, and harmony. He has appeared on *Oprah*, CNN, and many other TV shows; and his work has been featured in *USA Today, New Age Journal,* and *Newsweek* magazines. Mr. Robinson teaches workshops and speaks to corporations, associations, and churches around the country in the areas of peak performance, communication skills, and practical spirituality in the workplace. He is the author of four other books, including *The Little Book of Big Questions* and *Communication Miracles for Couples.*

If you have a story to share about how you've integrated work and spirit, if you would like free information about Mr. Robinson's talks and workshops, or if you'd like to receive a free catalog of his various audio- and videocassettes, please write, fax, or e-mail:

Jonathan Robinson
278 Via El Encantador
Santa Barbara, CA 93111
(805) 967-4128 (fax)
e-mail: IamJONR@aol.com

NOTES

NOTES

NOTES

We hope you enjoyed this Hay House book.
If you would like to receive a free catalog
featuring additional Hay House books and products,
or if you would like information about the
Hay Foundation, please contact:

Hay House, Inc.
P.O. Box 5100
Carlsbad, CA 92018-5100

(800) 654-5126
(800) 650-5115 (fax)

Please visit the Hay House Website at:
www.hayhouse.com